A Cup of Comfort

for Friends

A Cup of Comfort

for Friends

Stories that celebrate the
special people in our lives

EDITED BY
COLLEEN SELL

ADAMS MEDIA CORPORATION
Avon, Massachusetts

Published by
Adams Media Corporation
57 Littlefield Street, Avon, MA 02322. U.S.A.
www.adamsmedia.com and www.cupofcomfort.com

ISBN: 1-58062-898-2 (hardcover)
ISBN: 1-58062-622-X (paperback)

Printed in the United States of America.

J I H G F E D C B A

This publication is designed to provide accurate and authoritative information with
regard to the subject matter covered. It is sold with the understanding that the publisher
is not engaged in rendering legal, accounting, or other professional advice. If legal advice
or other expert assistance is required, the services of a competent professional person
should be sought.
    —From a *Declaration of Principles* jointly adopted by a Committee of
    the American Bar Association and a Committee of Publishers and Associations

Cover illustration by Eulala Conner.

This book is available at quantity discounts for bulk purchases.
For information, call 1-800-872-5627.

Where love abides, friendship thrives
With love and gratitude to
Paula Munier, Sherri Lindloff, and Judy Sebille
My lifelines, my friends

~

Acknowledgments

All books are collaborations. An anthology such as this, especially, requires the combined and orchestrated efforts of many talented people, and I am deeply indebted to them all.

Kudos and my hearty thanks go to each of the authors who contributed their wonderful stories to this celebration of friendship. I also extend my sincere thanks and good wishes to all those who shared stories with us that we were unable to publish in this collection.

The staff at Adams Media Corporation has gone above and beyond the call of duty in making this book a reality and a success. I am most grateful for the support and guidance of publisher Bob Adams, director of publishing Gary Krebs, and managing editor Kate McBride. For their dedication, hard work, and camaraderie, I sincerely thank the editorial staff, past and present—particularly Kate Epstein, Laura MacLaughlin, Gloria Jasperse, Leah Bloom, and Jennifer Lantagne—as well as the dynamic publicity duo of Gene Molter and Sophie Cathro.

I would be remiss in failing to thank Paula Munier for

bringing me into the Adams fold, for her pivotal role in creating *A Cup of Comfort*, and for her friendship and professional partnership of nearly twenty years. She is one of the universe's shining lights, and I thank the stars every day for her presence in my life.

I humbly thank the loved ones behind the scenes who inspire and support me 24/7: my parents, siblings, children, grandchildren, dear friends, and funky dance and life partner, TNT. They make everything possible and worthwhile.

Bless you, gentle Readers, for joining us for this cup of comfort. Cheers!

Contents

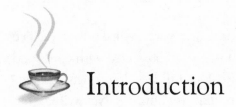 # Introduction

*Friendship is precious, not only in the shade, but in the
sunshine of life.*

—Thomas Jefferson

To have a friend is a blessing. To be a friend is an honor.
Yet, as friends, we are typically relegated to standby status
in one another's lives. Oh, we do our best to connect
when one of us has something significant to celebrate or
commiserate. Otherwise, though, we tend to squeeze each
other into whatever slots are left over after the other
people and responsibilities in our lives get their share.

Amazingly, our friends understand. They patiently
wait their turn and graciously accept whatever time and
attention we give them. They're always there when we
need them, and they forgive us when we're slow to recognize their needs. Such is the nature of friendship—true
friendship.

Still, as author Pam Brown said, "A friendship can
weather most things and thrive in thin soil; but it needs a
little mulch of letters and phone calls and small, silly presents every so often—just to save it from drying out completely." I love that quote. And I love exchanging little

goofy, sentimental, personal gifts with my friends. My office is filled with them: a hand-painted box filled with cards and letters from friends; a two-foot-tall wooden toucan; paperweights; bookends; a miniature antique typewriter that holds my business cards; several Irish mementos, including a framed four-leaf clover and a hideous ceramic leprechaun; bookmarks; dozens of well-chosen books; candles; photographs; a gardening plaque; a collection of stones and rocks from around the world; a miniature Irish cottage; a handmade glass fountain pen; a ballet wall calendar and a writer's desk calendar; a framed poem, "A Writer's Blessing," penned by fellow scribe-triber, Paula Munier; and other treasures.

The real treasures are the people who gave them to me. As much as I enjoy and appreciate every single memento, I value what they represent more. Their gifts say that these lovely people love me. In the midst of their busy lives, they think of me. They've made the effort to know me, to reach out to me, to make memories with me—not out of duty or familial fate, but because they chose me. They chose me to be their friend. What an honor. I get misty-eyed at the mere thought, and the incredible miracle, of that. The real gift is their friendship.

Somehow, my reciprocal gifts of carefully selected items, whether simple or extravagant, don't seem quite enough. Neither do my greeting cards, letters, e-mails, phone calls, visits, and occasional helping hand. I think of my friends far more often and they mean much, much more to me than these expressions of friendship convey. I vaguely remember a pop song (not my usual cup of tea) that asks, "How do you thank an angel?" How, indeed.

"If the only prayer you ever say in your entire life is thank you," wrote thirteenth-century sage Meister Eckhardt, "it will be enough." When it comes to friends, we usually reserve our thank-you's for the things they do for us, usually in our time of need. It seems to me that recognition for the experiences and relationships that our friends share with us is long overdue. It really doesn't matter how we express our gratitude—only that we do. Let's start today.

This little collection of true stories about real friendships is our way of honoring, celebrating, and giving thanks to those special people in our lives: our friends. We hope you'll enjoy these fifty wonderful stories about true friends—and that you'll share this cup of comfort with yours.

—*Colleen Sell*

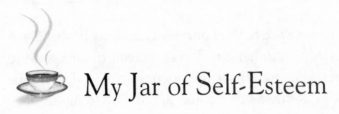 My Jar of Self-Esteem

Karen and I met when our first children were both eight months old. She was a new member of the church in which my husband was a pastor. We soon discovered that we had a number of things in common: a favorite shade of blue, a passion for obscure hymns, similar wedding bands, and a mutual faith.

As a pastor's wife, I'm usually friendly with the people who attend the churches that my husband serves, but I usually don't form deep friendships with them. However, when I met Karen, I knew immediately that she saw me beyond my role in the church and that I could trust her.

Our instant bond strengthened as our lives continued to run parallel with one another's. Karen's three children were born within two weeks of mine. Our friendship grew with our families, forged on barfy pregnancies, colicky babies, and early childhood illnesses. Our husbands both worked long hours, and so our daily phone calls became our mutual lifeline, a connection to reality filled with laughter and reassurances that we would live through whatever challenges life presented us.

Just before the birth of our third child, my husband was transferred to another city. It was difficult to say good-bye to Karen, but we knew our friendship would continue somehow. Neither of us could afford daily long-distance phone calls, so at Karen's suggestion, we did "one-ringers." Every afternoon when the kids were down for their naps, I would make myself a cup of tea, call Karen, let it ring once, and hang up. Karen would have tea ready at her end, dial my number, let it ring once, and hang up. That way, even though we couldn't talk, we could still enjoy our tea together.

About that time, my middle child decided that she was never going to sleep again . . . ever. I had a four-year-old who wanted to play all day, a nineteen-month-old who wanted to scream all night, and a baby who wanted to eat constantly. I dreamt about sleep the way starving people dream about food. Sleep deprivation eroded how I viewed the world and myself. I couldn't think clearly. I couldn't have reasoned myself out of a damp paper bag. The left side of my face twitched for two years.

Karen couldn't offer me sleep or a helping hand with my children, but she helped lift my spirits with two thoughtful gifts. The first came in the mail: a pretty flowered mug filled with my favorite tea. On the wrapper of each tea bag, she had written a different verse of hope and encouragement that I was to find in my Bible and read while we had our tea times together.

A few months later, when Karen's husband was in town on business, he brought me another package. It was a beautifully decorated ceramic quart container with a label that read, "Sig's Jar of Self-Esteem. Use as necessary," with a prescription to apply whenever I doubted myself or felt lonely. The jar was packed with slips of fancy pale blue paper, rolled into capsule-sized scrolls, each containing a message just for me. There were dozens of them.

> *God smiled at me when He sent me a special gift named Sig.*
> *I treasure your friendship.*
> *I'd love to live within 100 feet of your kitchen.*
> *You are raising kids that will be well-equipped for life.*
> *You have the gift of hospitality.*
> *I appreciate your consistency.*
> *You are the person I would most like to be stranded in a mall with, provided it had a daycare and a German coffee shop.*
> *I really believe you could do anything you wanted.*

In beautiful calligraphy, each little blue "pill" reminded me that I was special, that I had gifts to offer, and that I was loved. I laughed and cried as I read the notes. The first night, I almost overdosed on them. The jar found its way to the kitchen, where I could reach for it just before my face started to twitch.

Fifteen years later, my jar of self-esteem still has a special place in my heart and in my kitchen. I don't use it as often as I used to; apparently the magical potion of friendship helped to rebuild my self-esteem. The twitching returns only when I don't get enough rest, which is quickly rectified by a dip into my jar of self-esteem.

I now work full-time, so we no longer do the one-ringers, but we can now afford the occasional phone call. She and her family visited our home recently, and over steaming cups of tea we discussed, among many other things, the future. We called our teenaged children into the room and asked them to please promise us that, when Karen and I can no longer make decisions for ourselves, they will place us in the same nursing home. They agreed. It dawned on us afterward that we hadn't planned for our husbands, who are also friends, to join us. We decided that they could come, too.

—*Sigrid Stark*

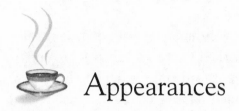 # Appearances

I stood at the top of the windy hill, my ankles throb-bing, snow flurries whipping my hair, my warm breath fogging up my sunglasses. And I started to cry. Of course that only made things worse, and I had to take off one of my wet woolen mittens to remove my glasses and wipe at my eyes.

I looked around at the other skiers swishing down the mountainside in their coordinated pastel or racing-stripe ski overalls and parkas. In my jeans and blue turtleneck sweater, with only a long-sleeved leotard and tights, rather than thermals, underneath my clothes, I stood out like a sore thumb, and I was freezing. My rented boots and skis were ill fitting. My clothing was not waterproof. I had no idea what I was doing at the top of that mountain or how I was going to get down.

All these people could afford to have fun, I thought. They had the latest equipment, the trendiest clothes. Most of all, they had each other. I did not fit in.

I was a scholarship student in my senior year at a pri-vate college in Southern California. My boyfriend had asked me to go skiing with him and his friends for senior weekend. When he'd asked me to go, I had felt so privileged. Now I felt that it had only widened the chasm between the other, affluent kids at school and me. They'd been skiing since they'd started walking. They could go skiing on a whim with no regard for the cost. They'd all been born with silver spoons in their mouths. I hated them all.

My boyfriend was different. His parents could afford to send him to college, but they were middle class, at least. Even though his friends were wealthy beyond my imagination, he acted as though he fit in. I hadn't a clue how to act like them. I was a poor girl from the valley who had won a Ford Foundation minority scholarship to an exclusive college. The trip was just a further reminder that I didn't belong.

I'd already fallen five or six or seven times; I'd lost count. I had to get down the mountain somehow, so I decided to try skiing again. I angled in the tips of my skis to snowplow as I'd been taught in the beginner's ski class that morning. I shifted my weight to the inside of my heels, pushed off with my poles, and headed straight down the mountain, out of control and screaming with fright.

Suddenly, the path ahead curved sharply. I'd never been taught to turn and was about to head off the slope into unknown territory. At the last moment I purposefully fell to my right. My momentum carried me down the slope and into one of the large padded pillars that formed the base of the chair lift. It snagged my ski and miraculously stopped my downhill tumble.

I managed to get to my feet and stood there shaking for a few minutes. The entire right side of my clothing was soaking wet. My left ski had come off and, fortunately, was only a few feet from me. I took off the right ski, retrieved the left ski, and holding the skis in my arms, began trudging down the slope, totally defeated.

"On your right!" someone screamed. "Get off the run, idiot!" Skiers yelled choice epithets as they zoomed past me. I ignored them and continued walking.

I kept looking around in hopes of spotting my boyfriend in his dark green parka. An intermediate skier, he had kindly paid for my morning beginner's ski class. In fact, he had paid for the entire weekend: equipment, lesson, and lift tickets. We were staying with the parents of his roommate at school. Of course, he was also the one who'd taken me up the chair lift to an intermediate run, yelled "Good luck!" and then abandoned me so he could ski with his fraternity buddies.

A guy in a navy blue parka and matching ski pants swished to a stop in front of me. His skis were personalized with the name "Theo," and his yellow ski boots gleamed with newness. I didn't know him but was grateful that anyone would stop to help. He pushed his sunglasses on top of his head and glared at me.

"You aren't allowed to walk on the runs. You could get killed." He pulled his shades down over his eyes and barked, "Put your skis on!" as he skied away.

I numbly walked to the edge of the slope and plopped down. I realized I didn't even remember exactly how to tell the difference between my right and left skis. I don't know how long I sat there staring when a hand tapped me on the shoulder. I would have jumped with surprise if my limbs weren't stiff with cold. All I could do was turn and look.

"Are you okay?" the figure asked in a strained feminine voice. I saw that she had on a beautiful powder blue ski outfit with matching leather gloves. Another ski bunny, I thought bitterly.

I tried to say, "I'm fine. Please go away," but my voice rasped unintelligibly. The woman reached into her fanny pack and came up with a bota bag. She offered it to me.

"It's just water," she croaked. "My throat always gets irritated when I ski." She laughed hoarsely. "My voice doesn't always sound like this."

I nodded and took the bota bag. As the cool sweet water comforted my mouth and throat, I smiled for the first time that morning.

"My name is Diane," she said. "I'm sorry, I think I've seen you at school, but I can't remember your name."

"Lynda," I said, certain she'd forget it in a minute. I remembered her from school. She was in a sorority and had plenty of friends. "Thank you for the water," I said politely as I stood up and started to put on my skis.

Diane steadied me as I slipped my boots into the ski bindings. It took a while, and I finally worked up the nerve to ask her if my skis were on the right feet.

"Yes. They usually put an *R* and an *L* on beginner's skis, but these are intermediate skis. Are you a beginner?" she asked.

I was embarrassed to admit my lack of knowledge. "I

finished a lesson this morning," I replied with more indignation than I intended.

She laughed and said, "You must be pretty tired. You'll have to take it slow and easy on the way down and try to stay to the side, out of the hot doggers' way."

I nodded and decided to fess up. "I can't. I don't know how to turn. I only learned how to snowplow."

Diane's eyes grew wide with shock. "You mean you only took the bunny beginner's class? You shouldn't even be on this slope!"

I cringed at the vehemence in her voice, realizing that she was just another person who felt I didn't belong there. I started to put on my wet woolen mittens, but they were frozen. I shoved them into my jeans pockets and picked up my poles. I felt so ashamed of my appearance and ineptitude. I didn't look Diane in the face when I muttered, "Thanks anyway."

She didn't respond, so I looked up and saw that she was staring down the slope. She had pushed back the hood of her parka, and her long, curly red hair fluttered in the wind. I knew she was looking for her friends, trying to find an excuse to abandon me.

She turned back to me and smiled. "We can do this, together. It's only intermediate for a few more turns and then it gets easier."

I shivered and began to cry. Not because I was cold. Not because I hurt all over. Not because I was humiliated. But because someone was willing to help me when I needed it.

Diane took some tissues out of an inside pocket and handed them to me. I blew my nose and wiped my eyes.

"Thank you," I said, looking directly at her so she'd know I meant for more than just the tissue.

She took off her powder blue gloves and handed them to me. She pulled some thin leather gloves out of another pocket and put them on her hands. "My driving gloves," she said in explanation.

Then she took off her parka and handed it to me. I shook my head.

"I have layers of thermal clothing on, and you don't. Now, put this jacket on!" she scolded with a smile.

I did, and in a moment we were off. She guided me slowly down the hill. She taught me the basic snowplow turn as well as how to traverse and how to stop. It took us nearly an hour to finish what was normally a ten-minute run. But we were laughing with cheery exhaustion when we finally made it down to the lodge.

I noticed my boyfriend and his buddies in line for the ski lift. He waved at us. "Come with us for another run."

Diane and I looked at each other and laughed, shaking our heads no. We took off our skis and sat outside the lodge watching the skiers. I tried to think of a way to thank her but didn't know what to say or do for someone like her, who seemed to have everything.

Then she said, "Thank you so much."

I couldn't help laughing. "I'm the one who should be thanking you for saving me from freezing to death on the side of that mountain!"

She sighed. "You know, my family takes all this for granted: the warm clothes, the private lessons, the two-week vacations." She looked at me. "Don't get upset, but

I'm glad you were stuck up there today. It's great to meet someone who faces a challenge and doesn't expect to be handed everything on a silver platter."

At that moment, I knew that we'd continue to learn from each other, to help each other, to share joy and sadness together, to be friends for life.

That was twenty-eight years ago, and we've remained good friends. Diane now lives in Utah with her husband (I introduced them!) and their child (our godson, Daniel!). She and her family visit me and mine in southern California at least twice a year. We rarely go skiing.

Finally, I've found a way to thank my redheaded snow angel.

—Lynda Kudelko Foley

Dumpster Roses

The invitation was on expensive parchment paper engraved in gold. It read: "Nothing but the best, for the best." I shivered with excited anticipation at attending this reunion of my dearest college friends, being held at the home of one of my oldest childhood friends.

I rose early the Saturday of the reunion. The five-hour drive sped by as I reflected on the changes in our lives over the past twenty years. Kathy was running the campaign for a senatorial candidate on the East Coast. Jim was a college professor and a successful writer. Gina was the only one from our acting group who was making a living in theater. Mike, a close friend since childhood, was the senior vice president of a large marketing firm. I was a high school special-education teacher, the first in our group to marry, and the only one to have more than one child.

Driving down the shaded lane to Mike's resort-sized, waterfront log home, I was impressed by the brilliant gardens that accented the beautiful property. I remembered his note that he had hired a full-time gardener.

That afternoon and evening were as wonderful as I

had anticipated. We windsurfed and swam in the lake, and the ten of us talked and laughed late into the night. The next morning Mike and I carried our coffee out to his greenhouse; he wanted to show me the long-stemmed roses his gardener was nurturing. Glancing at me casually across the scarlet beauties, Mike dropped a bombshell.

"You know, Lou, in college you had more potential than any of us. We all expected you to be more than just a mother and a teacher."

My delight in our reunion drained out of me. Was this what my old friends thought of me, that I didn't measure up to the rest of them? I struggled to keep my composure, too rattled to respond. I headed for home as soon as I felt I could politely leave. After hugs and sworn statements that we would do better at keeping in touch, I was on the road. Given Mike's comments, I questioned their sincerity.

I'd never spent much time analyzing my life; I'd always been too busy. Now, I prayed all the way home, "Lord, have I used my talents correctly? Are you disappointed in me, too? Please show me whether I'm living the way you intended."

When I arrived home, my four children gifted me with hugs and a sincere interest in the details of my weekend. I was relieved that I didn't need to teach the following day. I was attending a conference, and a substitute teacher would be in my classroom. I looked forward to the chance for some quiet reflection.

I had promised my kids that I'd introduce the substitute before I left for the conference that Monday. Ms. Smith,

the substitute, arrived late, even though I'd asked her to
be early so I could prepare her. Racing down the hallway
to my classroom with a gasping Ms. Smith trying to keep
up, I attempted to give her a quick rundown on each student. Upon reaching my tiny, windowless classroom, we
were greeted by fourteen agitated students, all eager to
talk with me.

"Mrs. Zywicki, they want you in the office," said one
student, Kandi, who was eager to add to the barrage.
"Sandra got in trouble in her group home, and she's
banging her head on the wall."

Tina's partially unzipped duffel bag began to wail. The
fifteen-year-old mother gingerly scooped out her two-
month-old daughter, her pleading eyes meeting mine.
"Sorry, Mrs. Z. The babysitter showed up drunk this
morning. My dad is coming to get Angel at nine o'clock,
when he gets off work."

I nodded at Tina and turned to the boy with the bright
blue, Statue of Liberty hair. "You're my man today, Pete,"
I said. "Introduce Ms. Smith here and tell her how we do
things."

I gave Ms. Smith a quick I-know-you-can-do-this pat
on the hand and turned to leave.

"Mrs. Zywicki, wait! I've got to talk to you before you
go down to the office," pleaded red-haired, chalk-faced
Kandi. "I broke out of detox this morning, so you mark me
absent, okay?"

"We'll deal with this tomorrow," I said with a sigh
before I clipped off to the office, the sharp heels of my
dress-up shoes echoing down the hall.

Ten minutes later, I was back, resigned to the fact that the conference would begin without me. "Where's Ms. Smith?"

"Don't know," said Pete. A circle of fourteen faces smiled in innocent agreement. "I did everything you said. I introduced everyone. We shared the best thing that happened to us over the weekend, like we always do on Mondays. And we started reading the short stories that we wrote last week, just like you told us we were going to."

"Ms. Smith looked like she was going to puke, and she left," Kandi added. "Don't know what the problem was."

I picked up the phone and canceled my spot at the conference, then notified the office that Ms. Smith had disappeared. At the end of our difficult day, the vice principal stopped in for a minute.

"Thanks for sticking around today, Lou," she said, smiling. "How does it feel to be indispensable?"

I threw her an amused, yeah-right look.

"Seriously, though, those kids need you. I'm glad you're on our staff."

Then she was gone as quickly as she'd come. I sent up a silent prayer of thanks for the much-needed compliment. Exhausted, I continued to sit at my desk, deep in thought.

Two dearly familiar faces stuck their heads around the doorway and asked if they could come in. Before I could answer, Kandi and Pete came in carrying a bouquet of exquisite, long-stemmed red roses. "We're sorry you missed your meeting because of us, Mrs. Zywicki. We found these in Rick's dumpster and thought you would like them."

The two teens stood silently, their eyes fixed on my face. I could sense some sort of tension hanging between us, but I didn't know where it came from. I waited.

At last Kandi broke the silence. "Mrs. Z, most people are afraid of kids like us. They don't want to be around us or to teach us. You like being our teacher, but more than that, you're a true friend." Her eyes held mine as she struggled to get out her last three words: "We love you." They each gave me a quick hug and took off, escaping the heavy emotion they'd just heaped on my lap.

I stroked the satiny red petals of my magnificent roses. "These are far more beautiful than the ones in your greenhouse, Mike," I said quietly to myself. But as I spoke, a huge tear fell on the back of my hand. My heart ached with both thankfulness and pain. I wanted my old friends to recognize that my job was every bit as important as any of theirs, and maybe someday they will. I also realized something more important: that my job is important, that my life is filled with true friendship, and that I am exactly where God wants me to be. He showed me with a bouquet of dumpster roses.

—*Lou Killian Zywicki*

Providence Provides

M aggie was in my life for such a short time that I would wonder whether she was only a mirage were it not for a little wooden napkin ring. I use it at every meal, and I remember her.

She appeared one April morning, fresh as the first breeze of spring. I will never forget my surprise when I opened my door to find a tall, willowy girl with fresh-scrubbed skin glowing with health, blond hair gathered in braids, and a gingham dress flowing in the midday sunlight, like an illustration straight out of *Little Women*. A complete stranger to me, her simple beauty reminded me of the Quakers, and her soothing voice comforted me.

I'd been meaning to place an ad in the newspapers for a housecleaner, but I hadn't yet gotten around to it. When I asked how she knew I needed someone, she said that she "just knew."

I'd lived alone for forty years, and despite a history of physical limitations, I'd always managed to do most of my own housekeeping. When I did need a hand with something, I could always count on nearby friends or neighbors to help. Three years before, however, I'd bought a home and moved to a new city where I knew no one. I lived on a quiet street in a conservative town where neighbors minded their own business. I didn't know the telephone number of the couple who lived on the east side of my house, and the large family on the west side was often drunk and always angry at my barking dogs. Now, I'd reached the point where I needed help not only in emergencies but also with everyday chores.

Just when I needed her, there stood Maggie. I asked about her experience. She admitted that she'd never cleaned other people's homes professionally before, but that she'd had plenty of experience cleaning her own. I questioned whether she really wanted to clean houses for a living, whether she wouldn't be happier doing something more interesting, something with her mind. Married with two young children, she explained that she wanted to earn money fast so that her family could move away from the frenetic San Francisco Bay Area, maybe buy some rural property up North. Then she took my hand, and I knew before she spoke her next words that I'd hire her.

"I'm not afraid of hard work, and I like to help people. My master's degree is in social work. I worked in a hospice for a while and loved it. After that, I was a home hospice nurse, and I enjoyed caring for the patients and their families, but I couldn't stand taking money from people who were dying. It didn't seem right."

"Well, I'm not dying, and my house is filthy," I said. "How much do you charge?"

"Whatever you pay," she said.

That was how our relationship began, but it quickly

transcended that of employer/employee. Maggie often thought of me as her mentor, and I always considered her my friend. We traded life experiences, and confided our deepest beliefs and longings. We frequented museums and galleries, attended concerts together, and went on walks and on picnics with her children. She felt and treated me like family. As I look back on that time, I cannot help but believe that some higher power sent Maggie to me.

The previous year, I had attended the Edinburgh International Festival in Scotland, spending every dime I'd scrimped and saved during the entire year on airline tickets, accommodations, and a full schedule of plays and concerts. I was planning to return and had made all the arrangements before Maggie had come into my life. I was to leave August 8th and stay until Labor Day.

The last week in July, as I hurried out to water the backyard flowers and reached for the faucet, I tripped on the hose and fell against the stucco wall of the house. I sunk to the ground in pain. I couldn't move, I couldn't cry out for help, and I lost consciousness. The next thing I remember is hearing Maggie's voice.

"Lynn Ruth! Where are you?" she called from the doorstep. She must have spotted me, because within seconds, she was at my side. She lifted me up, helped me to her car, and drove me to the hospital.

It wasn't Maggie's day to clean my house. She'd been in the neighborhood and decided to drop by unannounced to give me some apple butter she'd made the night before. She arrived less than five minutes after I fell.

Four hours later, I was in a plaster cast and in my own

bed. I had broken my shoulder and cracked the two bones in my upper arm. Maggie stayed with me in the emergency room and drove me home. I couldn't cook my dinner, take a bath, or walk any farther than the bathroom.

"What will I do about Scotland?" I'd asked the doctor. I had all the tickets, and it was too late to cancel them.

"I'll give you pain pills, and I'll change the cast right before you leave," he'd said. "We have ten days to get you mobile, and I think we can do it, if you do your part and take it easy."

What I didn't then realize was how much of a part Maggie would play in my recovery. We never discussed the extra demands on her time, and she refused additional money for it. When I awoke, Maggie was there beside me. She cleaned me up, fed me, and settled me in my bed with a good book before she left to take care of her other clients. She was back at six o'clock to prepare my evening meal and tidy up my house. At ten, she returned in her pajamas to check on me and settle me in for the night. We talked and laughed, helping to heal my spirits and my body.

On August 7th, the two of us returned to the doctor. He gave me a lighter cast and the green light to go to Scotland. Maggie took me to the airport and saw me off on my three-week cultural adventure. While I was gone, I exercised my arm gently and slowly regained some use of my torn muscles and broken bones. By Labor Day, I was able to walk down the jetway unassisted—and Maggie was there to greet me. She drove me home to an immaculate house, a filled refrigerator, and a delicious dinner. Above the front door, she'd hung an immense banner decorated with butterflies and flowers, and shouting, "Welcome home, Lynn Ruth!" Inside, the table was set with a lovely floral placemat and a matching napkin drawn through a cheerful kitten-shaped wooden napkin ring that she'd purchased for me.

The next day I cooked for myself and drove to the market. Later, Maggie stopped by.

"I have some news," she said. "I can help you this week, but after that . . ." She took my hand. ". . . Bill and I found some property outside Yreka, and we're moving there next Sunday."

My tears of sorrow in losing her mingled with my tears of happiness for her in following her heart. I squeezed her hand.

"I'll manage," I said. "Will you write to me?"

"I'll call," she said. "I'm a terrible letter writer."

She never did. And I never saw her again. I found someone else to clean my house. Though my shoulder continued to ache, I was able to take care of myself. I missed Maggie's sweet presence, but I no longer needed her. Had she not been there after my fall, I would have been hospitalized and alone. I doubt if I would have healed enough to go to Scotland. Maggie helped me to continue my life, and she brought sunshine into my life. Then, as magically as she'd appeared on my doorstep, she was gone. I like to think that providence sent her to someone else who needed her more.

Since then, I've tried to be a Maggie to others whenever I can. It is my way of saying thank you to the heavenly spirit that guided Maggie to me when I needed her most and called her away when I needed to stand on my own.

—*Lynn Ruth Miller*

Thelma Rae

Thelma caught my attention with a wave of her arm from the beach just below me. Blue jeans rolled up to her knees, she sat with her bare toes digging into the warm sand as she worked. Her curly hair, having fallen victim to the coastal wind, whipped across her face. At thirty-six years old, she looked as much a teenager as I did, and even with the eighteen-year age difference between us, she had long been my best friend. Waving again, the tablet fell from her lap as she motioned me to join her.

A strange way to spend an afternoon for some, for us it had become almost a tradition. Thelma and I shared a love for writing, and Simpson Beach was an inspirational place to work. We would each bring our tablets and find a comfortable seat. Then, sitting apart to avoid the temptation to chat instead of write, we worked separately, yet in unison, as the waves crashed and the seagulls sang around us. Offshore in the sea, a large wolf-shaped rock watched over the scene—"Wise Old Timmons," Thelma called him.

I climbed down from the ledge ten feet up the base of a sandstone cliff, where I had been nestled with my tablet.

Work time was obviously over; now it was time to play.

I joined Thelma in the warm sand; our tablets were soon forgotten as we ran along the water's edge, splashing in the waves. Like two kids we threw pieces of driftwood into the surf and waited for them to come back. Then we headed off to visit the tide pools, located at the edge of the rock cliffs on the south side of the beach. Thelma loved to gently poke the tiny sea anemones with her finger. I seldom dared touch them, but it was fun to watch them suck their long, sticky tentacles into a soft wad of color attached to a rock. Sometimes we also found starfish and tiny crabs, which we'd hold for a moment before releasing them to return to their pool. Every visit to Simpson Beach was full of new discoveries, and it was always an afternoon well spent.

There were also many nights that we sat up until dawn just talking. It was no wonder we were best friends. We had so much in common: an affinity for Chinese food and soft music, the Oregon coast, and, of course, writing. Sometimes during our long talks Thelma would get philosophical and offer advice about life. She taught me that every now and then, grown-ups do say things worth listening to.

"It's better to have it and not need it, than to need it and not have it," she often said. It was just one of countless axioms she was fond of. I don't know whether she made the little phrases up or if she read them somewhere, but even today they echo through my mind at just the right moments.

When I was old enough to date, she told me there are two things to remember when searching for that perfect guy, your soul mate. The first one was, to truly judge a man's character, watch him around children and dogs. If he takes the time to show them affection, he will do the same for you. It seemed silly back then, but it also made sense.

"Second," she said, "you will never find a perfect man, so find one with faults you can deal with."

I wondered at the time if she ever thought about looking for her soul mate. Years before, she had lost her husband of ten years in a logging accident. She had been single ever since.

I finally met the right guy, and at age twenty-five, I got married. Though the time that Thelma and I spent together lessened, we always stayed close. Early in my marriage, I had a daughter, and Thelma was with us in the delivery room. She breathed through the contractions with me for fifteen hours, and she held my hand while they stitched me up after my daughter's birth. I named her Tessa Rae, giving her Thelma's middle name. I'll never forget Thelma's beaming face as she repeated the baby's name over and over again.

Things got harder after that. My husband accepted a job three hours away, and we had to move. Thelma's health had been poor for a while, and I worried about her daily, but we faithfully stayed in touch. I tried to coax her into moving closer, but she resisted. Then one day she called me at work from the hospital.

It was cancer, terminal, because they hadn't caught it in time. The phone nearly dropped to the bakery floor as I fumbled, in shock, to keep it to my ear, those words thundering through my head.

"I'm on my way," I heard myself whisper.

"Can you bring some of those lemon-filled donuts?" she answered. Picturing her dancing blue eyes pleading, I almost smiled.

The hospital was quiet when I arrived that evening, but Thelma's room was full of beeps, buzzers, and strange faces. I put on a brave face as I walked into her room. There was Thelma, her usual vibrant self, sitting high in the bed and teasing the nurses. Next thing I knew, she was lecturing me about keeping positive.

The cancer traveled quickly from her lymph nodes to her bones and then into her brain. I held her hand daily, watching her fade slowly. My brilliant, articulate Thelma could barely speak.

During our last visit, she couldn't say much, but I know I saw a smile when I sat Tessa Rae on my friend's tummy in the hospital bed. Thelma weakly lifted both hands to play patty-cake one last time. Then I retold old stories of Simpson Beach to eyes so blue and now so hollow.

Now, I embrace those memories. I pass the stories, along with the words of wisdom—my friend's legacy—to Tessa and her brothers. I also try to write regularly, and to eat Chinese food and visit the Oregon coast as often as I can. You see, Thelma was extra special. Not only was she my best friend, but she was also my mom.

—*Tisha Coiner*

Side by Side

My first day of kindergarten in 1965 brought more than a few jitters. Not only was I leaving the familiar surroundings of home, I was also about to become the first black student in a predominantly white, Lutheran grade school. Though my parents were Baptists and my hometown of Racine, Wisconsin, had several public schools with integrated student bodies, my parents liked this particular school's academic and religious disciplines. After several meetings with the principal, they felt comfortable with their decision to send me to the Lutheran school.

Our family had friends of many races, and we lived on a street with friendly neighbors of Spanish, Armenian, and other cultures. But at school I would be the only African American among 320 students, two-thirds of whom were Caucasian. There were no demonstrations when we arrived at the school that first day, but I could sense my parents' apprehension in how tightly they each held one of my hands as we walked to my classroom. My teacher, Mrs. Lueckfield, greeted us with a warm smile and gently assured us that all would be well, and my parents had carefully explained ahead of time how my first day of school might be. Still, when I peered into the classroom at the sea of unfamiliar and entirely white faces, I had a hard time letting go of my parents' hands. Mom and Dad kissed my cheeks and reassured me that they would see me again soon. Mom hesitated a few moments, then smiled and winked as she let go of my hand and stepped away. Dad kissed me again and promised me lunch at McDonald's before pulling away to join my mother. As I watched them walk down the hallway, Mrs. Lueckfield smiled again, beckoned me in, and told me to sit at one of the child-sized tables.

The room was brightly decorated with pictures and live plants. Sunlight streamed in from huge windows on two sides of the room, and I could see a small playground with monkey bars outside. All of the kindergarten kids from both the morning and afternoon sessions, about twenty-four in all, were assembled together that first day. As I walked up and down the three neat rows of tables and chairs, trying to decide where to sit, they laughed and chatted noisily. A few paused to stare and point. I tried to speak, but fear strangled the words in my throat. My eyes filled with tears, and my heart pounded in my chest. I wanted my daddy, and I wanted to go home—right now!

Just as I turned to run out of the classroom, a soft voice asked, "Would you like to sit here?" The voice belonged to a girl with brown hair who seemed as shy as I was. I stared at her, blinking away my tears, questioning whether she was really talking to me. She asked me again, and I slid into the chair next to her. We grinned at each other and introduced ourselves. Then the sound of our voices chatting away blended with those of our excited classmates, until Mrs. Lueckfield called the class to order. When it came time to go to the church service, Diane and I walked side by side to the church and made a point of sitting together during the service.

My parents beamed almost as widely as I did when I told them about my new friend and all the fun I'd had my first day of school. The second day was nearly as good. When I walked into the afternoon kindergarten classroom, Diane excitedly waved at me to come and sit by her, and I happily ran to my seat. We played together at recess and shared the first of many secrets—our favorite colors. Hers was purple, mine pink. We even sat together on the school bus ride home at the end of the day. We quickly became inseparable buddies in our class of eleven afternoon kindergarten students.

Diane's friendship was one of the few bright spots in that trying year. Other kids made fun of my skin color. A few were afraid to touch me, for fear my darkness would somehow rub off on them. Others implied I was dirty and didn't bathe as often as they did. Some called me "nigger" and even hit me. Nearly every day, someone assaulted me verbally, physically, or both. Both Mr. Eichotz, the school principal, and Mrs. Lueckfield quelled these problems as quickly as they could, but it didn't stop the attacks. Through it all, Diane defended and supported me. Even when I took out my hurt and frustrations on her, we would quickly make up, and her friendship never wavered.

We were both saddened when the school year ended in June. Because we lived in different neighborhoods and attended different churches, we knew we'd be apart until school started in the fall. The only time we saw one another that summer was when Diane and her grandmother unexpectedly dropped by our house. I leapt with joy when Diane shouted my name as her grandmother's blue car turned onto my street. I left my friends and rushed to the car to talk to her. Both of us eagerly agreed to count the days until school started again. It seemed like an eternity.

When first grade finally arrived, we greeted each other like old friends, slipping into our camaraderie as if we'd never been apart. Of course, we both made other friends, only some of whom we shared, but we remained close throughout childhood—despite some tough challenges that the differences in our friends, neighborhoods, and cultures created.

Diane was often invited to sleepovers, parties, and other social activities to which I was rarely invited. Because the few kids on my street were either much younger than me or jealous of my parents' sending me to a private school, they usually didn't include me in their fun, either. Though my parents tried to compensate for these slights by talking things over with me and with fun family activities, being excluded by my peers hurt. It hurt a lot. I found comfort in reading and in my continuing friendship with Diane.

As adolescents and teens, Diane and I talked on the phone nearly every night, about boys, homework, our hopes and fears, our likes and dislikes. I learned to rock out to Led Zeppelin, Yes, and Pink Floyd, and I laughed uproariously every time Diane sang "My Name Is Mikey" in a deep voice. She opened herself to my grooves, including The Brothers Johnson; Parliament; and Earth,

Wind and Fire. Though everyone knew Diane and I were the best of friends, I was still virtually the only black student in our school, and our best times were those shared alone together, free from social and parental constraints.

Soon after high school graduation, we both left town. I went off to Marquette University in Milwaukee, and Diane moved to Memphis, Tennessee. A year later, she returned to Racine. Although Milwaukee and Racine are less than an hour's drive apart, our lives moved in separate directions, and our visits were sporadic. While I contended with the rigors of college, Diane worked as a bookkeeper at a local produce market. On my few trips home, Diane was one of the first people I saw, and we'd always talk, laugh, and connect as if we'd seen each other only the day before.

Music and mirth aren't the only things that sealed and strengthened our friendship. It has been sharing tough times, along with the good times, that has molded us into sister-friends in the deepest sense of the word. At age twenty-three, I was severely injured in a near-fatal car accident soon after I had moved to Grand Rapids, Michigan, to work as a newspaper reporter for a local paper. When I was released from the hospital and moved back into my parents' home in Racine, a very pregnant Diane was one of my first visitors. A few months later when she gave birth to a healthy baby boy, Ryan, I was by her side. When my parents died within three years of one another, leaving my brother Eric and me to care for our mentally handicapped brother, Diane pitched in to help us whenever we needed her and was my constant comforter. When her marriage crumbled, I was there to lend a hand with Ryan, whom I love like a son, and to offer my unconditional support.

Our friendship has remained a constant in a sea of change. In 1994, I moved to Los Angeles to resume my writing career, with Diane's complete, if tearful, support. She celebrates my every literary victory and encourages me to follow my dream. Three years ago, I rejoiced when Diane's dream came true and she married the love of her life, Doug. I was her maid of honor, and felt so grateful to Doug for bringing security and happiness to both Diane and Ryan. When I find that special man to call my husband, Diane will be by my side with the support only a sister-friend can offer.

Sometimes, Diane and I are amazed at how intricate a part we play in each other's lives. Our friendship is like a lighthouse in a storm, anchoring and guiding us as life whirls all around. While our love and caring for one another have grown with each passing year, the bond between us has matured in ways we never could have imagined in our youth. Yet, on Diane's visits to California and on mine to Wisconsin, we act like schoolgirls again, overjoyed with the pure pleasure of just being together. Today, on the eve of our fortieth birthdays, we still feel blessed by this sisterhood-friendship that began thirty-five years ago with a shy little white girl inviting a shy little black girl to sit next to her on the first day of kindergarten. In my heart and in spirit, Diane and I will always sit side by side.

—*Marcie Eanes*

A Tale of Two
Snowflakes

I grew up on a dairy farm in west central Wisconsin. One year, a stray white cat showed up in our barn. I was fascinated with the white cat—mostly, I suppose, because all the rest of our barn cats were tabby or gray or black. A few weeks after the white cat arrived, she gave birth to four kittens. Two of them were white.

I was so enchanted with the white kittens that I could scarcely wait to show them to our elderly neighbor, Hannah Paulson. I knew she liked kittens as much as I did. Our farm and the Paulson farm were the only residences on a mile-long stretch of country road. Since we had no neighbors with children and no other children in our family for me to play with (my brother and sister were twenty-one and nineteen years older than me), during the summer I'd ride my bicycle down the hill three or four times a week to visit Mrs. Paulson.

Hannah, who was in her seventies, always wore checkered aprons over cotton shirtwaist dresses. Sometimes we gathered flowers from her garden, because she loved to have fresh flowers in her house. Sometimes we just sat at the kitchen table and talked. At other times, I helped Hannah feed her outside cats. When they had retired, Hannah and her husband, Bill, had purchased the farm next to ours and inherited with it a number of cats, most of them wild. That didn't stop Hannah from trying to make friends with them. Occasionally, she even succeeded.

One day after the stray cat's kittens were big enough to drink from a dish, I loaded the two white ones into a box, put the box in my bike basket, and headed down the hill toward our neighbor's place.

When Mrs. Paulson opened the front door and saw what I'd brought, she seemed at a loss for words. She just smiled and motioned for me to come inside. I set the box down on the living room floor, picked up the kittens, and turned to Hannah. Still without saying a word, she held out her hands. I carefully placed a kitten in each of her palms.

"Oh, dear," she said, gazing at the two white balls of fur. "Aren't you just the sweetest little things."

She lifted her hands close to her face and kissed first one kitten on top of the head and then the other. The kittens didn't even look surprised. They were used to being kissed on top of the head.

"What are their names?" Hannah asked.

"Uh . . . I haven't decided yet."

That was really quite odd. Usually I'd have picked out names for kittens by the time they were old enough to start drinking milk from a dish. But in this case, all the names I'd thought of until then hadn't seemed quite right.

Mrs. Paulson nodded. "Finding just the right name for each of them is important."

She started to lean forward. Then she straightened up again and held the kittens out to me.

"You'd better do it," she said. "I'm not sure my knees will hold."

I put the kittens on the braided rug in front of the door. They huddled together and looked around uncertainly.

Hannah smiled. "I know what you'd like," she said, gazing fondly at the kittens. "I'll bet you'd like some cream."

When my neighbor trilled "kitty-kitty," the kittens immediately focused their attention on her. They knew very well what that meant, and they scampered after Hannah as she limped toward the kitchen.

My mother had told me that Mrs. Paulson suffered from arthritis in her knees and that was why she sometimes had trouble moving around. During my visits, I had noticed that as time went on, her knees seemed to bother her more often. In fact, that summer she'd been going outside far less often than she used to.

As Hannah slowly made her way across the kitchen, she kept talking to the kittens, who followed along, gazing up at her with blue-eyed wonder. She took a container of cream from the refrigerator and poured some into a saucer.

"There," she said, turning to me. "Would you set that down for them, please?"

I put the saucer on the long braided rug in front of the kitchen sink.

"Kitty-kitty," I called. The kittens stopped nosing around Mrs. Paulson's shoes, which were made of brown leather and had thick, heavy soles. She said they were called "ortho-pedic" and made her knees feel better.

The kittens didn't wait for me to call them a second time. They raced over to the rug, sniffed the dish for a few seconds, and then eagerly began lapping the thick, white cream.

"I knew you'd like it!" Hannah exclaimed, clasping her hands together under her chin and smiling down at the kittens.

She turned to me. "Let's sit at the table. I don't know how much longer I can stand on these knees."

We sat and watched the two white kittens, still positioned one on either side of the saucer, lapping steadily.

"Just look at them. Aren't they precious?" Hannah said.

I knew our neighbor well enough to know that anything she described as precious was simply divine in her estimation.

Hannah sighed. "Those little darlings sure do bring back memories. Why, they look exactly like my Snowflake did when she was a baby."

I turned my attention back to Mrs. Paulson. "Snowflake? Who is Snowflake?"

"A white kitty I had when I was just about your age," she explained.

"And you got her when she was a kitten?"

Hannah nodded and began to stroke the woven straw placemat in front of her with the tips of her fingers. "That was when I was growing up on our farm in South Dakota. Snowflake was my best friend. She used to sleep with me. And I'd dress her up in doll clothes."

"You had a cat that would let you dress her up in clothes?"

Hannah smiled. "Snowflake even tried to follow me to school. I'd read her stories, too, and she'd curl up in my lap and look for all the world as if she understood precisely what I was saying. We did everything together. Until . . ."

"Until what?" I asked.

Hannah glanced at the kittens, who were finishing up the last of the cream. "Until she died."

"Oh."

Mrs. Paulson focused her gaze on the window above the kitchen sink. She had a faraway look in her eyes. "We figured Snowflake had eaten a poisoned mouse. My mother had put out strychnine, because she didn't want mice in our attic. I cried for days."

A lump rose in my throat. I knew what Hannah meant. I remembered how I felt when my friend, Momma Kitty, had died a few years ago.

I looked across the table and saw that Hannah's eyes were filled with tears.

She sniffled and took off her wire-rimmed glasses. "Now, isn't that silly of me?" She shook her head as if to clear it of the memory. "That was ever so long ago." She reached into the pocket of her apron for a tissue, so she could wipe her eyes and blow her nose.

When the kittens finished licking the saucer clean, Hannah crumpled a piece of notepaper and tossed it onto the floor. The paper ball bounced on the blue and gray tiled linoleum and rolled toward the cupboard. The girl kitten watched it for a moment and then pounced on it. Her brother promptly joined in, batting it from beneath his sister's paws.

I'd never watched kittens play with a paper ball, and I giggled so hard I almost made myself sick. Hannah laughed, too. It was good to hear her laugh, because I knew it meant that she wasn't thinking about Snowflake anymore.

After a while, when the kittens grew tired, they curled up together on the rug in front of the sink and fell asleep.

"Wore themselves out, didn't they," Hannah observed, gazing at the kittens. She looked over at me. "I haven't laughed so much in years. Thank you for bringing them."

A short while later, it was time for me to go home.

"Where are the kittens?" my mother asked when I walked into the house. "Did you put them in the barn?"

I shook my head. "No . . . no, they're not in the barn."

Mom gave me a quick, sharp glance. "What's the matter? What happened to the kitties?"

"I— I— "

I stopped and drew a deep breath. "I gave them to Hannah."

My mother stared at me, eyebrows raised. "You did what?" she asked. "But you love those kittens!"

I told her about Snowflake and how Hannah had cried. I didn't like to see anybody cry, but especially not someone as nice as Hannah.

"So, I thought maybe she'd like to have the kittens," I explained.

Then without warning, I began to sob. "I don't know why I gave my kittens away, Mommy! How could I do such a thing?"

"Sweetheart," Mom said, holding out her arms. "Come here."

My mother gave me a long hug. Then she pulled me around to sit on her lap.

"I'm so proud of you," she said.

"Why?" I asked, my face pressed against her shoulder.

"You gave Hannah something you love, because you thought she needed it more."

Mom stroked my hair. "Hannah's knees are bothering her quite a bit this summer," she said. "Have you noticed that?"

I nodded.

"She hasn't been able to go outside like she usually does to work in her garden. She hasn't gone to Ladies' Aid meetings, either. Sometimes when I talk to her, she seems kind of sad. I imagine those kittens are going to be very good company. They'll be sort of like medicine, to help her feel better."

I lifted my head to look at Mom. "Like medicine?"

She smiled and gave me another hug.

Even though my mother seemed to think I'd done the right thing, I still wasn't quite sure what had possessed me to give away my white kittens.

But in the following weeks as I watched my friend Hannah lavish love and attention on the little cats she named Snowflake and Snowball, I began to understand.

—*LeAnn R. Ralph*

In Praise of
Temporary Friends

I have always envied other women's friendships. It's not that I don't have friends. I do. But I don't have a friend I can call at four in the morning, who would hop on the next plane to come hold my hand through disasters great and small. I don't have a friend I've known for so many years I can't remember life without her. I don't have a friend who knows all my secrets.

I've read about such friendships: the YaYa sisterhood and Judy Blume's summer sisters. I've seen them on the silver screen: Bette Midler and Barbara Hershey on the beach, Thelma and Louise driving over the edge of the canyon, hand in hand. But this is the stuff of fiction and melodrama. These are not real women, women like me, who've moved eight times and lived in six states since high school, shedding friends with each move; who've had to forego friends for kids because there wasn't time to be true to both; who've always kept their own counsel.

Yet I know that deep, abiding friendships do exist. Recently, I read a story about five women who have been meeting for dinner once a month for twenty-seven years, and for a moment I was flat-out jealous. I cannot imagine the stability of a group friendship like that, the sense of history—the marriages and divorces, births and deaths, toddlers and teenagers—they must have shared, the comfort, the security. I will never have that.

But I have had something else, a kind of friendship that may be even more miraculous. It is a sudden, intense friendship born of adversity, a fierce, temporary connection that comes when you need it and fades when the moment has passed. When it is happening, it is the most important relationship in your life. When it is over, the hole it leaves closes quickly.

Nancy was the only person I could think of to call when I got the news that there was something ominous on my mammogram. I knew there were many things it could be, but I also knew there was only one thing it was. The biopsy, a day later, confirmed my suspicions. Nancy was not a close friend, but she was the only one I knew who had had breast cancer.

"Damn!" she said over the phone, a reaction I came to appreciate later after two close friends fell apart when I told them. What you don't want when you tell people you're facing something terrible is pity. You've got enough of that going on inside. What you do want is anger. There is energy in anger.

Nancy came over that afternoon and sat with me at the kitchen table for hours. I don't know what she did with her two children. I don't know how, over the next two weeks, she rearranged her life so that she could be a fixture in mine. I never asked, and she never burdened me with the details. During those weeks, other friends called; other friends cared. But they didn't know what to do. "Call me if you need anything," they would say, meaning it. Of course, I didn't. I couldn't articulate what I needed. I didn't know what I needed. Nancy knew.

Nancy is a large, solid woman who listens carefully and measures her words. She is not a hugger, but when she hugs, you stay hugged. That first afternoon she sat and listened, occasionally pouring more tea, as I railed on about death and dying, how I couldn't believe this was happening to me and how I would never live to see my kids through middle school. When she got up to leave, she took hold of both my hands and looked me in the eyes. "I'm still here," she said. "You will be, too."

The next morning she dropped by to lend me her cell phone so I wouldn't be housebound waiting for calls from doctors and labs. Later that day, she drove me to my first appointment and sat with me as the surgeon outlined the reasons he couldn't do a lumpectomy and would have to remove my breast. When he left the room and I allowed myself to cry, she sat next to me on the examining table, her shoulder touching mine. "Do you want to see what a mastectomy looks like?" she asked. I nodded, and she lifted up her shirt, unhooked her bra, and showed me.

I found myself calling her several times a day. Sometimes, I had news. "I have estrogen receptors!" I yelled once from a pay phone. That was good news, because it made the cancer more treatable. But sometimes there was nothing new to report. I just wanted to hear her calm, soft voice.

She came with me to all my appointments that first week, tape-recording the sessions in case I missed something, handing me paper cups of tea, keeping me fortified with cartons of yogurt. She insisted I go for a second opinion and arranged everything for me, making appointments with the doctors in Seattle who had treated her four years earlier. She took two days out of her life to come with me—to drive five hours each way; to stay in a motel; to sit with me in waiting rooms, exam rooms, and consulting rooms; and when it was all over, to celebrate my "excellent prognosis" with something sweet and gooey from the bakery.

Then, as quickly as she'd come into my life, she left it. She was in charge of a two-week camping trip for her daughter's school. She had to go. By the time she returned, I had weathered a few storms on my own. My surgery was over and so was the initial shock. I was less needy. I was more myself. She sensed that immediately and slipped back into her life, her children, her husband, her work, her own set of friends.

I saw Nancy a few times after that, and for a while we spoke weekly on the phone. "Just checking in," she would say. Then the phone calls, both hers and mine, grew less frequent and finally all but stopped. She went back to being what she was before, a person I occasionally saw around town.

The problem with temporary friendships is that you don't get a chance to repay the debt. I think of those five women who have met for dinner every month for nearly three decades and all the opportunities they've had to return each other's kindnesses, to trade places, needy and needed, over the years. Nancy and I don't have that history nor will we have that future.

Once, in the thick of our two-week friendship, I despaired aloud over never being able to adequately thank her. That's when she told me about Janet, who came from nowhere to pull Nancy through the three worst weeks of her life. "You are how I'm repaying Janet," she said.

So it is that temporary friendships outlast us, repeating themselves serially, rhythmically, as each of us steps up when we are needed. We temporary friends are shamelessly intimate. Our connection is white hot, too hot to last. But it is also too essential not to pass on. I know how I will thank Nancy.

—*Lauren Kessler*

The Old Basque and the Young Jew

A wounded animal hides in its den. That is what I did following a traumatic marriage and divorce: I moved to a small town and hid from life. As a caseworker for the Department of Health and Welfare, I was surrounded by strangers in need and coworkers I kept at a distance. At home, I kept to myself. My only close friends were the furry ones with whom I shared my house. I might still be in that sorry state had it not been for a courtly, elderly Basque who led me gently back to life.

Tony first came to my office on a particularly crazy day. It was my job to conduct interviews with everyone who applied for welfare; I also did crisis intervention and provided information and referral services. Some days were quiet, with only a handful of clients. Others, I might see fifteen or twenty people a day. Tony first appeared on one of the latter days.

I'd already had a steady stream of complicated problems: transients who couldn't afford to fix a broken-down car; a family that needed food stamps immediately but didn't have an appointment; a recent widow whose grief was compounded by the discovery that her husband had no pension; a scared pregnant teenager whose parents had thrown her out of the house. So, when a tall, dignified, silver-haired gentleman ushered a small, nervous-looking Hispanic woman and two children into my office, I didn't expect what followed.

"This is Luisa Cruz," he said in fluent, accented English. "She needs to apply for welfare, but doesn't speak English. I came to help her."

I sighed with relief. I was just too tired to struggle with my poor Spanish. With the man's help, we completed the interview quickly and efficiently. Then, my next client arrived, and I forgot about Mrs. Cruz and her friend.

That night, I went home to my silent house and collapsed on the sofa. My cat snuggled next to me with a soft purr. "Sam, I can't stand it," I moaned. "Some days I see too much trouble, pain, and loneliness. I give, give, give. No one gives to me—except you." Sam purred louder, but he wasn't much comfort. I burrowed my head under the cushion and cried.

I was twenty-seven years old and alone. I'd moved to Israel after college, married at twenty-three, and divorced the same year after my husband had become violent. I returned to the United States and attended graduate school, moved to a remote town where no one knew me, and began working at the welfare office. My ordeal with my ex-husband had taught me about life's seamy and sorrowful sides, so I empathized with the clients. But I had a tremendous distrust of men and couldn't imagine dating, let alone ever marrying again. Besides, there were no Jewish men in the small town I'd relocated to, no possibility of falling dangerously in love.

The seasons rolled by. I spent time with casual friends. I rejoiced when one coworker became engaged and when another had a baby. But my heart remained heavy in my chest.

One day, the stately gentleman came back into my office, alone and carrying a sheaf of papers. "I'm Tony Ramirez," he began. "I came about a friend."

He explained her situation, and I realized that, with a couple of phone calls, I could probably solve the problem. I jotted down the details and asked for his number so I could let him know what I found out.

"I don't have a phone," he said. "I'll come back in a few days."

True to his word, Tony soon returned. I'd solved his friend's problem, and after giving him the good news, we chatted for a few moments.

"No," he said. "I worked for the railroad. But I speak good English, and I like to help people."

A few weeks later, he was back with more questions about the affairs of his elderly friend. He returned again and again, each time with a different question. His friend's problems had very easy solutions, and I didn't understand why such a bright, articulate man kept bringing them to me.

One day, my secretary said, "That Mr. Ramirez looks in the door sometimes, and if we're busy he goes away. What does he want?"

I realized with a shock that what he wanted was to visit me.

The next time he came, he again began by explaining his elderly friend's troubles. When he paused, I said, "Mr. Ramirez, you don't need an excuse to visit. My job is to talk to people. If no one is waiting to see me, you can just stop in to say hello."

His handsome face flushed, and for the first time he was at a loss for words. Then he nodded. "You are a smart lady, missus."

"Hanna," I said. "Please call me Hanna."

"I'm Tony, Hanna." He pronounced my name with a guttural *ch*, the Israeli way, and I liked it. "You're a smart lady. You knew an old fool like me just wanted a chance to talk with a pretty young lady."

After that, Tony became a regular visitor, never staying more than fifteen minutes. He had a thousand stories, yet he was also a good listener. Without realizing it, I told him a lot about myself—my early dreams and their derailment; about living in a community where there were no single Jewish men.

One day, St. Anthony's Hospital called: Tony had been admitted. I was puzzled by the call, but after work that day and several more times until he left the hospital, I sat by his bed and we talked. Once the nurse asked if I was his daughter. "No," I said. "I'm just a friend."

"Oh," she replied. "I'm glad he has you. No one else comes to see him."

How could it be that a person who had done so much for so many people was so alone, I wondered.

A few weeks later, he was back at my office. "I want to tell you the story of my life," he said.

"Okay," I replied. It was a slow day, and we had plenty of time.

"My name, as you know, is Juan Antonio Ramirez," he said. "I'm Basque. I grew up in the Pyrenees Mountains near the French border. We spoke the Basque language at home, and I learned Spanish and some French in school."

He described his early days, helping his father herd sheep. He learned to estimate the weight of a stack of hay and how the weight varied from the fall, when it was fresh, to the spring, when it had settled down under the winter rains. He spoke of coming alone to America as a teenager, of herding sheep, of buying and selling hay. Eventually he became a conductor on the railroad.

"I traveled across the West," he said. "In those days, railroads were the only way to travel; the trains were full of people. I was tall and handsome, and my European manners made them feel like royalty. I had a woman in every city: Salt Lake, Las Vegas, Los Angeles. Sometimes women passengers would invite me into their roomettes for a liaison. Sometimes I'd have a few days off in Los Angeles, and a lady passenger would invite me to come to her hotel. I was a fine dancer, and the big bands played wonderful music. I had a good life."

He was silent for a few moments. Then he leaned forward. "Hanna, I never married. I had money; I had excitement; I had all the fine women I could want. In those days, I thought that was enough; I thought I didn't need anyone." He reached into his shirt pocket, pulled out a huge wad of bills, and fanned it so that the hundreds and fifties flashed by my eyes. He shrugged and stuffed the money back in his pocket. "Now I am old, and I am all alone."

Would I be like that someday, old and all alone? The thought chilled me. I didn't want to become a sad, lonely old lady who filled her days by talking to strangers on park benches.

That night, with Tony's words echoing in my ears, I pulled out my folder of unanswered letters and responded to them. Soon after, I quit the job that had become such a burden, and I began substituting in the public schools, surrounding myself with lively children. I looked for Tony to tell him, but I didn't find him.

One day, driving through an unfamiliar part of town, I stopped at a stop sign. Crossing the street directly in front of my car was my distinguished old friend.

"Tony! I haven't seen you in ages!"

"Hanna, why are you still here?" The disappointment in his voice surprised me. Though he had spoken of going to Mexico, I had never mentioned moving away.

Tony reached into his pocket and handed me a silver ballpoint pen. "Here, Hanna. Write me a letter when you've moved on."

Reaching for the pen, I realized that he was right: I had to leave. If I stayed, I, too, would one day be old and alone. I looked down as I blinked away the tears that flooded my eyes. When I looked up again to ask for his address, he was out of sight.

I was determined to turn my life around, but I was still afraid of letting anyone get close to me. Being scared was no excuse for remaining in a protective shell. Hadn't Tony told me how scared he was, when as a fifteen-year-old boy he'd come to America? His first job was buying hay. He soon realized that since Idaho haystacks were a different size and shape than Basque stacks, he had no idea how much they weighed. He certainly couldn't figure out the difference between fall and spring weights. Yet, he'd carried on and eventually mastered the trade. Later, he'd built a successful career with the railroad.

Many of his stories, I suddenly realized, had been about overcoming fear. At thirty-one, I was more than twice the age he'd been when he'd arrived in America. If I moved to a bigger city in another state, I'd still be in my own country, speaking the same language, living in a similar culture. How hard could it be?

Within a few months I had sold my house, moved, and begun my journey back to life. I wanted to write Tony to let him know and thank him, but he hadn't given me his address.

More than twenty years have passed since I last saw Tony, and I'm sure he is no longer living. Over the years, I've thought of him often. I missed him most at my wedding. He would have liked my practical, down-to-earth husband.

—*Hanna Bandes Geshelin*

Names of clients have been changed.

Summer Solstice

The answering machine's blinking light is the first thing I see as I enter my home. The apartment is small, and I can see the light as soon as I open the door. Buffy, my blond cocker spaniel, hurls herself from the over-stuffed couch and dances at my feet. I let her lick me until she is sated, and then she returns to her still-warm nest.

I stare at the answering machine. I'm still not sure how I feel about it. While I don't want to be reminded of my obligation for the night, the promise of a familiar voice seems like tonic to my lonely soul.

I throw my overburdened key ring onto the counter. It lands with a loud slap before sliding to its resting place in the corner. There are small scratches in the blue Formica from years of what I like to call key bowling. Sometimes Michael and I would take turns, earning a point for perfectly wedged keys. I can still hear him say, "You're the man, Mom!"

I wonder if they know today is his birthday.

I glance again at the blinking red light. It draws me like a beacon.

I push the play button, and a soft, tentative voice fills the room.

"Hi, Melanie. Call me when you get in."

The caller didn't leave her name; she didn't have to. She knew that I'd know it was Chessie, sweet, copper-haired Chessie with the perfect smile and the large blue eyes. Chessie, who tonight at the bar will appear aloof until maybe her third drink, after which she will lure even the lowest life forms to our table just for fun.

I smile. I love Chessie. And I love April, Rita, and Debra, too. But today is Michael's birthday. It would be wrong to join them.

The next message is from Rita, glib, honey-voiced Rita, whose heart is bigger than her body. "Hi, sweetie. Call me when you get a chance."

Then April. She hasn't bothered to turn down the music, and Janis Joplin competes and wins over her message.

I wonder why there isn't one from Debra.

The girls. We still refer to ourselves that way, although we are women now.

I close my eyes and remember the day I returned home from the maternity hospital to my cramped, second-floor apartment with the rickety staircase. Michael was wrapped in a thick blue blanket, and I cradled him protectively. After two days of round-the-clock nurses and visiting relatives, I ached to have him all to myself. I had just put on my slippers when the doorbell rang. If it had been anyone else, I would have resented the intrusion. I opened the door, and there they were. My heart rose like a balloon.

They aren't company; they're closer than family. They are an extension of me.

Chessie, generous Chessie, brought me a box of white knit baby clothes that I know she was saving for herself but insisted I keep.

Rita, maternal Rita who dreams of having five children, took Michael from my arms and refused to part with him for almost an hour. She shut herself in his small yellow nursery, and when I stood at the door I could hear her singing. This made me cry a little, and I said a prayer that I would be as good to Michael as Rita would be to her children.

April, perpetual gypsy April, glanced at the infant, cooing, "Oh, you beautiful darling!" in her adopted southern accent as she poured the wine. "I guess we're all gonna have to smoke on the balcony," she said.

Rita, serious Rita, finally emerged from the nursery and whispered, "He's asleep." She accepted the wine from April but didn't drink it, not until she'd put fresh sheets on my bed, filled the diaper stacker, and made iced tea.

And Debra, effervescent Debra who was still in high school, came later bearing a homemade book of coupons for babysitting, story reading, and diaper changing.

The phone rings again, pulling me roughly from the comfort of my memories.

I do not answer, but instead watch until the red light flashes. I know it must be Debra.

I walk to my bedroom and remove a worn scrapbook from the nightstand. On its cover *The Girls* is written in red nail polish. I lay on my stomach, and my feet hang over the bed.

The first picture is of Chessie and me, round-bellied toddlers wearing identical pink bikinis and standing in front of a wading pool.

Chessie and me at five, six, ten, twelve.

Then it's Chessie, April, and me, looking gangly and awkward. April's blond bangs are cut too short, and she seductively juts her hip while smoking a candy cigarette. Chessie and I make the peace sign. I remember that after this photo was taken, we shared a Winston Gold that April had pinched from her grandmother.

A wrapper from a Three Musketeers bar is wedged between the pages. It's still sticky.

Then, a small school photo of Rita. Her thick, dark hair is styled into frizzy curls, and it's obvious that her mother has given her a perm. Under it are the words *New Girl,* in letters clipped with pinking shears from magazines. There is a snapshot of Rita in her candy striper uniform. Her sister Debra is dressed in a pink corduroy jumper and wears pigtails.

As we grow older, we grow closer.

Junior year homecoming . . . I didn't want to go, because I was doubling with Chessie and she was golden in her satin strapless and I was dull in my pale lace. I felt plain next to Chessie. My mother said Elizabeth Taylor would feel plain next to Chessie, and then the doorbell rang and she pushed me toward the door. The boys pinned on our corsages, and Chessie's came out of a clear plastic tube and mine out of a large white box from the florist. Hers was small and wilted, and mine was a tight cluster of fragrant pink roses, and then everything was okay. The next day my stomach knotted with guilt at having felt jealous of Chessie. I made a small bouquet with my roses and brought it to her.

Senior year. April didn't have a prom date, but she told us she didn't want to go anyway. I told her that she was my date, and Chessie brought Rita. Although Debra was only a freshman, she went with a handsome football player. But she was not one of us yet, so we ignored her.

The shrill ring of the phone makes me jump, and this time I answer.

It is Chessie.

"Hi," she says. I know she means, "Are you coming?"

"Hi," I say, and she knows I mean, "I'm not sure."

An unusual silence falls between us.

"April is flying in from Boston. Debra can't make the restaurant, but she's coming later. Rita finally got a sitter," she says.

I'm torn. I've spent the first Friday of summer with the girls for the last eight years—our own solstice. Our night. We always drive out to the Jersey shore for an early dinner, pick a seedy bar to nest in, and then walk the beach carrying silver-tipped sparklers until the sun comes up.

We've been doing it since the summer we turned twenty-one. Debra was there, too, using a copy of Rita's ID. If anyone thought it strange that both dark-haired girls were named Rita Ginardo, they never said.

Chessie says, "It won't be the same without you." Her voice is soft and liquid.

Guilt hits me like a fist, and I wonder how I could have thought even for a moment that they wouldn't know that tonight's summer solstice falls on what would have been Michael's ninth birthday.

Chessie, fragile Chessie, who cried so hard when she drove me home from the hospital that even through my grief I wondered how she could see the road.

Rita, hollow-eyed Rita, who lost so much weight from her grief she had to buy new clothes.

Debra, strong Debra, who told me she'd had a fight with her husband, the same football player from senior prom, and could she crash on my couch. I saw through the ruse, but lonely and scared, I said, "Sure." She stayed for two months.

And April, unconventional April, who gave me a puppy, as if a puppy could replace a dead son. She was so earnest, and I knew she would gladly have taken my pain and made it hers, and I held the puppy to my chest until it was wet with my tears.

I realize that Chessie has stopped talking and is covering the phone with her hand. I can hear her small gulping noises, and then I'm crying, too. We weep almost silently into the phone and not for the first time I think of her as my lifeline.

Buffy pads into the room but does not join me on the bed. Instead she looks at me mournfully with her deep brown eyes, and I wonder how she always knows when it's six o'clock.

"I have to feed Buffy," I say, breaking the silence.

"We don't have to go out," she says. "We could come to your apartment, drink some wine . . ."

"No," I say. "I need to take a shower, but I'll be ready soon."

I wait for her to break the connection before I put down the phone.

I follow Buffy into the kitchen. She holds her silky tail high and wags it, as if she's leading a parade.

I sit with her on the floor and watch her eat. I talk to her, but I'm really talking to myself.

"Buffy," I say, "I'm not forgetting that summer solstice falls on Michael's birthday. Or that my life is lying in scraps at my feet. But right now, what matters is that they're insisting I be there, because the night truly won't be the same without me."

And it won't.

She looks up briefly from her bowl and licks my face. I think she understands.

—*Christine M. Caldwell*

What Dreams
Are Made Of

"Luuuuke!" my daughter Allie exclaims loudly from the living room. "Mama, Mama, he here! Luke here now!" She runs unsteadily toward the front door, her shiny black shoes clattering loudly on the tile floor. She pauses to tug at her new red velvet dress, patting the logo as if to make sure Winnie the Pooh is still there. Crowing with excitement, she struggles briefly with the front-door latch, and when it gives way, she claps her hands, proud that she has mastered the troublesome latch at last. Surging forward onto the wooden deck, she strains on tiptoe to catch sight of her friend. Peeking coyly through the wooden railing, she catches sight of Luke waving excitedly from his seat in the Aerostar van parked in the driveway below. Luke, grinning from ear to ear, opens the window to respond, "Here I am, Allie, here I am!"

Luke bounces impatiently inside the van until his mother slides open the door to free him. Fifty pounds of exuberant energy, he bounds up the steps to our deck, waving merrily at Allie the whole time. Together at last, Allie and Luke hug excitedly and chatter about the activities planned for the day. Catching sight of me in the doorway, Luke makes a running leap into my arms. "Ice cream, Allie-Mom," he signs. I pretend not to understand, asking if he wants a glass of water. "No, Allie-Mom," he signs, "I want ice cream cone. Cold ice cream." I laugh and promise him a delicious treat after he's had his dinner. Reassured, he kisses my hand like a courtier before turning to wave good-bye to his mother.

Allie and Luke first met eight years ago, coming face to face on a patchwork quilt placed on the floor of a busy classroom in the foothills of the Sierra Nevada Mountains. Allie had been attending the special program for infants with developmental disabilities for two years; Luke was a year younger and had just moved from southern California. They were immediately attracted to one another and spent the next hour happily exploring each other's face with inquisitive fingers. Born with Down's syndrome, Luke and Allie had not yet learned to walk or talk. But they communicated easily with one another, rolling happily around on the blanket in coy games of hide-and-go-seek and steal-the-pacifier. Smiling, gurgling, and crowing, they brought smiles to the faces of teachers and parents alike. When the class was over, they would cry miserably and strain toward each other as they were carried out the door and tucked into car seats.

Today, Luke is the muscular one, the athletic busybody who likes baseball and hockey. He runs, jumps, and swings a bat with intense concentration and great vigor. An unabashed show-off, Luke likes nothing better than a stage and an appreciative audience. He bursts into song at every opportunity, clutching an imaginary microphone and waving his arms dramatically in the air. There are no strangers in Luke's life; he greets newcomers with a firm handshake and a big smile.

Allie is more subdued, preferring to watch new people and scenes for a while before joining in the fun. She loves to read and shares her newfound information with Luke by reading aloud from road signs. She injects a note of caution into their games. Climbing and jumping are not for her; she prefers a more studied approach, hanging onto the handrail as Luke leaps up the stairs.

Over the past eight years, Luke and Allie have forged bonds of friendship that transcend their disabilities and limitations. They interact easily, using a combination of body language, spoken speech, and sign language. Luke has a hearing impairment and wears specially made hearing aids. Knowing that he removes them frequently when they "buzz" in his ear, Allie checks carefully to see if he is listening when she has something important to say. Although both children can speak, they struggle to get out the right words. Both have used sign language since infancy to allow them to communicate without frustration. Allie's speech is more garbled, complicated by a stroke during an operation to correct a congenital heart problem. Out in public, she steps back while Luke strides forward to plunge into new situations.

Today, the two conspirators head for the large wooden toy box in the playroom. Their blond hair shines in the sun, and their blue eyes sparkle with the anticipation of shared games and mischief. Together, they construct elaborate fantasies peopled with cats, dogs, alligators, and gorillas. Luke puts on a long black fright wig and poses like a runway model, while Allie growls from behind her tiger mask. Luke grabs his Peter Pan hat and brandishes his sword to fight off Captain Hook. Allie laughs appreciatively, dons her silken butterfly wings, and joins him in a flight across the imaginary sky. Suddenly, they both shed their disguises and drop onto all fours. Allie is a small gray kitten, and Luke loudly barks his way toward her. Squeaking in mock fright, she crawls up onto the sofa. Luke joins her, and they laugh uproariously at their own daring.

"Food now, Allie-Mom, then ice cream," Luke communicates hopefully in a combination of sign and speech. Allie seconds his request with a gleeful cheer and hops around in excitement. They run to the bathroom to use the toilet and wash their hands. Faces gleaming and hands still dripping water, they come back and sit side by side at the dining room table. Companionably, they munch on grilled cheese sandwiches and French fries. Luke passionately urges Allie to try his chocolate soymilk; Allie solemnly signs "Yucky" and sips daintily from her glass of nonfat milk. "White is better," she signs. After eating their long-awaited ice cream, the two stack their dishes precariously and carry the piles to the kitchen sink.

Then they race back to Allie's bedroom to change into their swimsuits and head for the inflatable pool in the backyard. Reaching the wooden steps leading up to the pool, they discover that Allie has forgotten her sandals. Luke gallantly offers his arm, and they return to the house, signing "No shoes" when I ask them what they need. Five minutes later, they come out of Allie's bedroom with arm-loads of towels, sunscreen, plastic toys, goggles, flippers, and assorted paraphernalia. They stagger up the wooden steps to the pool once more, dropping their burdens onto the soft grass. Carefully and conscientiously, they arrange their towels side by side before slathering each other with sunscreen. Then and only then do they jump joyfully into the pool, sending waves of water sloshing over the side. I rest on a lawn chair in the shade near the fence, watching as they maneuver their flotilla of plastic boats and make imaginary milkshakes in the water. Luke tosses a foam rubber ball, which splashes water up into Allie's face. She grimaces in distaste, then grins and tosses the ball back at his chest.

Forty minutes later, both shout "Done" at the top of their lungs, while signing to me as if I just might be hard of hearing. I wrap each shivering body in a colorful beach towel and point them toward the blanket on the grass in a patch of sunshine. They head gratefully for the blanket, stepping gingerly across the prickly grass. Lying side by side, they laugh at some shared joke and kick their legs with joy. Then Luke jumps up, unable to be still for more than five minutes. "Come on, Allie," he says. "Let's have a bath!" They gather up their armloads of treasures and head down the wooden steps to the house.

An hour later, bathed and dressed in their soft cotton pajamas, they watch *Annie* on video as I read the news-paper. Luke sings along merrily, until Allie pokes him with an elbow and frowns at his intrusion. Subdued, Luke yawns widely and comes to sit beside me on the couch for a cuddle. Soon, Allie joins us, and I have a warm little body tucked under each arm.

"How about we go to my bed and read?" I ask. Instantly, the two buddies hop up and pull me by the arms to the bedroom. We climb up into my bed, where I am completely surrounded by a huge pile of books and two drowsy children. We read about all their old friends: Madeline, Clifford, Curious George, Peter Pan, and Captain Hook. Luke and Allie adamantly express their desire to try all the fun adventures in the books, although Allie isn't too sure she wants to join in the sword fight. Luke, however, vows to whip all of the pirates single-handedly. We read for another twenty minutes before Luke drops off to sleep; Allie hangs on for another ten, but then gives in and closes her eyes. Silently, I work my way free of their arms and legs and climb out of bed. Tonight, the two friends are together in the land of dreams. I kiss each sweet face and tiptoe out of the room.

—*Sandy Keefe*

 Pass It On

When I was about fourteen years old, my parents took me aside and hesitatingly told me I'd probably never go to college. As much as they wanted to provide tuition for my sister and me, it was out of the question due to my mother's heavy medical expenses. I looked at my mom's sad face and resolved never to bring up the subject again. Still, I had hope, and I carried it with me always, like a good-luck charm.

My father was a high school teacher and took extra jobs ushering at local ball games to pay for a few extras. Though Mom wasn't able to contribute to the family's income, she was a wizard at creating something special from little or nothing. She would take a few scraps of cloth here, adapt a pattern there, and sew up one-of-a-kind skirts and dresses for my sister and me. When we'd walk down the street in stylish outfits made just for us, it was hard to feel sorry for ourselves. Mom was so talented with various crafts that we never felt poor.

Still, when an older neighbor, Sharon, went off to college, a huge lump constricted my throat. I thought she was the luckiest person I knew. Seeing my strained expression, she suggested I look into scholarships, but when I did, I found out they usually paid for only a limited portion of tuition and expenses. My savings totaled $100, not even enough for one semester's books.

Soon, I was a junior in high school and busied myself babysitting for three different families. At a dollar an hour, the babysitting did little for my small bank account. College expenses seemed to increase each year by as much as I was able to put away. The fact that my father taught at my high school and helped students plan their college careers seemed especially cruel, but my mother's medical expenses were constant and my parents had vowed never to borrow money to meet them.

During my senior year whenever anyone asked about my college plans, I would break out in a sweat and mumble something about going to work instead. The empty words mirrored my feelings on the subject, but graduation seemed a long time away.

Near the end of the school year, my counselor called me to her office to ask about my post–high school plans. I fidgeted for a long time, then finally admitted there was little money for college and that getting a job seemed the only course of action. Then she asked me what type of job seemed likely. I stammered and stuttered as the realization hit me—hard—that I'd actually have to job-hunt in a few short weeks. When I lamented that I could barely type and had no experience, she said the only things I could do in an office were file and answer phones. She showed me the day's job listings; every single one of them required education or experience, or both—even for file clerks and receptionists!

She asked me what would I do if I had the resources to pursue anything I wanted. Without hesitation, Cornell University in New York popped out of my mouth. That's where my neighbor Sharon went, and her descriptions made the place seem idyllic, even if it was thousands of miles away on the other side of the country from my home state of California. In fact, every time Sharon came home, I could hardly wait to hear about her college life. In retrospect, I was probably a pest, but she never turned me down.

My counselor said that Cornell was far more than I could afford. Even with all my babysitting money, I had saved only about $500. She suggested a compromise: attend a local junior college at night and work part-time as a waitress during the day. That was a far cry from Cornell! I immediately put the preposterous idea out of my mind. I wanted the whole college experience of living in dorms, walking around a huge campus loaded with history, and attending classes in classic buildings taught by astute professors. I left having resolved nothing, with no clear plan for work or college.

I stopped by Sharon's house that night and spoke with her mother, Mrs. Echeverra, really just wanting to hear some news about goings-on at Cornell. I told her about the counselor's suggestion and moaned about my state of affairs. Mrs. Echeverra scolded me gently, saying I was better than someone who whined and complained, especially when my mom had done so much for me, often when she was ill. She was disappointed in me and told me so.

Mrs. Echeverra was someone we all admired. She was lovely and gracious, and, as I fully realized, she had looked out for my sister and me the many days my mom was sick. She'd taught me how to make chili, vegetable soup, and from-scratch spaghetti sauce, things my mom couldn't do. She'd also loaned me books and through her example had shown me how to make a warm, welcoming home. I felt terrible that she'd witnessed me wallowing in self-pity. I realized I'd done that a lot lately.

The following week, I visited Mrs. Echeverra to apologize and to tell her I'd found a waitressing job and registered for classes at the local junior college. Mrs. Echeverra said that if I completed my work there, I could probably get a partial scholarship to transfer to a state college. The rest of my expenses could be paid by loans and working more in the summer. Then she mentioned a special scholarship and said she'd see to the details when the time came.

Over the next two years I learned how hard waitresses work. My feet burned, and I was often bone tired. No matter how badly I felt, I had to smile and be friendly, even when customers snapped at me. To get through my coursework faster, I attended school full-time during the day, rather than at night as the counselor had suggested, and worked out a system of waitressing during the odd hours between classes. It was tough, but I wasn't alone. Many other students at the junior college also worked; some of the other girls were also raising children.

After graduating from junior college, I applied to the local state college and arranged for loans. With Mrs. Echeverra's help, I also obtained the scholarship she'd told me about, which provided just enough to make up the difference between what I had and what I needed. It wasn't Cornell, but the teachers were enthusiastic. Sharon put the frosting on my cake when she mentioned that some of her classes were huge and it was hard to speak with a professor. Not at my school! The University of California at Bakersfield had relatively small class sizes, and we worked directly with the professors, never a teaching assistant. Deciding I could easily forgo dorms, I instead shared a small apartment with a roommate. The campuses' many squat temporary buildings and palm trees weren't as picturesque as the ancient oaks and ivy-covered architectural masterpieces I'd envisioned at Cornell. Instead of rolling hills of manicured grass and shrubbery, there was a lot of dirt. The state college was, after all, built in the middle of oil fields, but the place fit the city's history of oil exploration and farming, and it seemed right.

Due to my work schedule, it took three years to do two years' work, but in time I finished college, framed my degree, and went off into the world, settling in the Midwest. Several years later while visiting my family in Bakersfield, I went into the financial aid office at the college. I was making my last loan payment and wanted to do it in person. I handed the clerk my check, and she brought up my records on the computer. When she realized this was my last loan payment, she congratulated me. I mentioned the scholarship and said what a help it had been, but she looked puzzled and said there was no record of a scholarship.

There must be some mistake, I insisted, and explained about the scholarship for teachers' children. She shook her head and said no such scholarship existed. I pressed her for details, but she was unable to provide any further information.

Mystified, I called the school the next day and spoke to another clerk. She, too, said I hadn't received a scholarship. After some prodding, she finally revealed that someone had made payments to the school every semester I was there. She said the person asked to remain anonymous and that was all she could reveal. But I knew.

Mrs. Echeverra had moved, and no one seemed to know where she'd gone. I had to find her. My family asked around, and we finally tracked her down in a nursing home. She was one of the livelier residents and remembered me on sight. We talked about our families and what we had done since we'd last seen each other. She quizzed me on my cooking skills, and I said that whenever I made vegetable soup or chili, I always thought of her.

Finally, I told her what I knew and that there was no way I could ever thank her enough.

She beamed and assured me there was: "When you find someone deserving, pass along a little kindness. That's the best way to honor someone you love."

—*Kathleen McNamara*

A Gift from My Ex

"Nice jewelry," I said to Pinky, admiring a new pearl ring on her finger. "Did Greg buy it for you?"

"Mr. Budget?" Pinky said, rolling her eyes. "Come on. You know how Greg is."

I know how Pinky's husband is. I used to be married to him.

After experiencing the trauma of our divorce, I never dreamed I would someday become friends with my ex-husband's new wife. True, Greg and I had been hopelessly mismatched. While some men and women are from different planets, Greg and I are from different universes. Sure, I wanted him to find a new partner, a woman who appreciated his finer qualities and tolerated the not-so-choice ones. But a year after our divorce, when Greg wanted me to meet his new bride, my insides quivered a little.

Most of my apprehension stemmed from the way the media nearly always paints the new wife as conniving and competitive. Pinky probably dreaded meeting me, too. After all, when has an ex-wife been portrayed as anything but a witch? Our assigned roles called for high animosity.

If we had followed the script, we would have both needed claws and fangs for the action scenes.

Despite our mutual misgivings, Pinky and I met each other. After five minutes, I understood why my ex-husband loved this woman. What wasn't to love? Smart, funny, kind, talented—the positive adjectives radiated from her. Instead of extending claws, Pinky proffered the torch of friendship. We parted with smiles on our faces and, for me, a calmer stomach.

Had Greg and Pinky run off together while he and I were still married, I'm sure I'd have felt differently. But by the time Pinky had come along, I had long since abandoned my claim to Greg. He was already on the block. Why resent a woman for bidding on him?

My first goal in my fledgling relationship with Pinky was to assure her that I had absolutely no interest in getting back together with her husband. That was tricky. I hesitated to voice my sentiments about Greg too directly, wanting not to trounce him as bad husband material. So, I brought up the names of new boyfriends as often as possible, and I talked about moving on with my life. Pinky soon saw that, apart from the kids, Greg and I no longer had a connection.

Pinky is different from me. That's why she gets along with my ex-husband. She knows how to handle him. During my marriage to Greg, when he hurt my feelings, I'd sulk or lock myself in the bathroom to cry. Pinky fights back—in one instance by dumping a bowl of tossed salad on his head. Pinky forces Greg to live up to his potential; I was too gentle on him.

There are other differences between us, too. Pinky is the only woman I know who volunteers to organize a jamboree with 1,500 Girl Scouts. The thought of arranging that many details makes me queasy. Pinky excels at cake decorating. She even made me a cake for my thirtieth birthday. I, on the other hand, once attempted a Mickey Mouse cake that my son mistook for a monster. When I contemplate dinner parties, I cringe; Pinky regularly hosts them.

Though opposites in many ways, Pinky and I found plenty to talk about. Having a spouse in common provided ample conversation. Once Pinky saw I wasn't scheming to get Greg back, she began sharing anecdotes that only an ex-wife could appreciate. Greg is legendary for squeezing the life out of pennies, and Pinky enjoys describing his reactions to her spending habits. She knows I will groan at the right places. Pinky even feels comfortable enough to telephone when she's especially angry with Greg to say half jokingly, "I can't take this man anymore. You want him back?" When I call Greg about a child issue, I secretly hope Pinky answers the phone. She and I can put in marathon phone conversations.

Other friends are baffled at this congeniality. In their experience, old wives and new wives do not go shopping together. The only place they appear together is in court. What a relief that Pinky and I don't need to hide when we see each other approaching on the street. Because of my children, Pinky and I have often shown up at the same award ceremonies, baseball games, and school plays. Why shouldn't we sit in the same row of the auditorium and chat?

Pinky loves my children. Though my kids did not always

appreciate Pinky, I always knew they were safe in her home—and well fed. She baked legendary dinner rolls and buttermilk brownies. She put together snack packs when they traveled between residences. My son even had me incorporate Pinky's chicken enchilada recipe into our menu rotation. Pinky and I were two different kinds of mothers; the children benefited from the positive aspects of us both.

Along the way, Greg and Pinky produced three off-spring of their own. Hallmark doesn't have a category for my relationship with those kids, but I feel like I'm some type of special aunt. They are welcome to stay at my house anytime, for a day or the summer. I've even attended some of their birthday parties and other special occasions. Their pictures are posted on several of my walls—after all, they are the siblings of my children.

I'm sure that being friends with me has been a sacrifice on Pinky's part. Perhaps she tires of the constant reminder that Greg had a life and a wife before she came along. Obviously, her lifestyle would be more affluent if Greg didn't have to pay child support to my household. Occasionally the situation is awkward for me, too. Sometimes I'll get an odd feeling when I'm standing in Pinky's kitchen, knowing it would be my kitchen if I were still married to Greg. Our friendship is a conscious choice, and the load on our hearts is lighter for having refused to be foes.

Pinky and I put our relationship to the ultimate test last winter: my daughter's wedding. Newspaper advice columnists feature weekly letters about feuding blended families at such events. I shed only tears of relief when Pinky showed up to help me with the preparations. She decorated tables, arranged food platters, set up the cake, and even brought me some bubble bath for postreception relaxation. As Pinky and I stood in the receiving line together, I knew that she deserved a grander introduction than "stepmother of the bride." Pinky's place in my life has been far more encompassing than that. When my ex gained a new wife, I gained a great friend.

—*Kathryn E. Dawson*

Holy Brothers

Growing up in suburbia was never quite the bliss our parents supposed it to be. To an idealistic kid with a thirst for adventure, the 'burbs meant miles upon miles of clunky strip malls, cookie-cutter houses, postage-stamp lawns—and boredom—for as far as the eye could see. But every place has its heart, the side known only to those who get close enough. And there is little that can draw a kid away from his neighborhood.

As a thirteen-year-old boy living on Long Island, New York, I found familiar comfort in my friends and in the secret kid places around our neighborhood. I knew all the best spots: the small parks and vacant lots, the best trees to climb and bushes to hide behind, the places where the sidewalk stuck up a few inches and you could "catch air" on your bike—and the longest way home when you weren't quite ready to go home.

It was February. Snow-packed sidewalks and barren trees lined the tidy streets. Thick icicles hung like crystal knives from the entryway of our house, symbolic perhaps of the piercing threat lurking within its silent walls. It was report-card day, and as usual I had failed to achieve a level of academic success that would satisfy my father.

I knew the routine. He'd stand over me and yell; I'd sit there and cry. He'd ask me if I wanted to be a garbage man when I grew up; I'd cry harder. He'd call me a bum, and I'd stand up, take a shallow breath, square my shoulders, and cry some more. Occasionally, he'd hit me. It was a routine I never quite got used to.

Between my school and home, there was a large field that led to a smaller park where we used to play football late into the sunburned summer evenings. I stood there, quietly trembling in the cold February mist. Fresh warm tears formed half-frozen puddles on my cheeks. Between my gloveless, reddened fingers I held my report card, like some sort of prophetic scroll. I was alone. Ron and Scott, my two best friends, had just left.

"Seriously, Jay," Ron said, peering at me through his thick glasses. "It won't be that bad. Honest." He placed his hand on my shoulder and smiled.

"Hey, our parents are going to be mad, too," Scott said. "But tomorrow, everything will be cool again. It's just some stupid grades."

"I don't know, guys," I said. "I have this feeling that this time is going to be really bad. I just don't think I can handle it."

They both just looked at me and shrugged their shoulders. What more could they say? What more could they do? Their earnest attempts to console me having failed, they trudged home through the snow, carrying equally unimpressive report cards.

None of us were good students, at least academically. But we were grand students of the imagination. Ron, always the overly excited kid in any group, was an avid action-movie fan. He constantly reenacted scenes and spent most of his day in a fantasy world where heroes existed and the good guys always won. Scott, usually the biggest kid in any group, also enjoyed acting out heroic and adventure fantasies. I, on the other hand, had a darker, more cerebral imagination, steeped in romantic rebellious fantasies on the lines of S. E. Hinton's *The Outsiders* and J. D. Salinger's *The Catcher in the Rye*. As I stood there alone in the park, I envisioned a life of nomadic wandering for the three of us—far away from report cards and angry parents.

I stood alone in the park until it began to grow dark, hoping the cold would numb the pain of failure. But as the slow shade of evening fell over the gray winter sky like a giant scarf, the freezing darkness made home seem more like the warm place it usually was—except on report-card day. And I knew it was time to face my father.

I took the longest way home, across the empty lots, over the school's track field, and finally back to the paved rows of well-lit houses. The brief respite of walking through the open terrain was replaced by the claustrophobia of suburban clutter. I walked past Ron's house, the blue flicker of a television flashing through the window. He was my oldest and most trusted friend, the one I knew would always have my back and would always be at my side, no matter what.

As I made my way home, a light snow began to fall, dusting the newly paved road. I turned the corner onto my street, and through the sparkling veil of snow I could make out our porch light, illuminating the driveway and revealing two cars, where I had hoped to see only one. From the moment I opened the door, I knew I was in big trouble. The kitchen was dark, and dinner had already been served. I walked into the living room, where my father sat alone, a crumbled copy of my report card on the table beside him.

He looked up at me and shook his head. "Sit down, son," he said, almost calmly.

I hesitated, and then slowly, my head bent down in shame, I walked over and sat on the couch beside him.

"Do you have anything to say for yourself?" he began, his tone perceptively more agitated than it had been a few seconds earlier.

I looked up at him, new tears welling in my bloodshot eyes. "No," I said softly.

"No!" he screamed, slamming his hand on the table and grabbing the report card. "Look at these grades! What the hell do you do in school all day? Sleep?!"

"No," I stammered between heaving sobs.

"'No'? Is that all you have to say for yourself?" he demanded. "What am I going to do with you?"

He placed his head in his hands before continuing. "Your mother and I have decided that it might be best for you to go to a private school, a military school."

I began to weep uncontrollably and pleaded with my father not to send me away. Without another word, he got up and walked away. I had escaped a spanking, but this felt much worse. I didn't know when or to where my father would send me packing, but at the bottom of my thirteen-year-old soul, I knew that I couldn't, wouldn't survive without my friends.

That night, I dreamed that Ron and I ran away together, hitchhiking on dark roads under starry skies to Florida, as far south in the United States as we could go—far from the pressures of school and home.

The next day I met Ron at the park. The air was frigid, but the sky was perfectly clear, like the hollow inside of a blue-domed cathedral. As soon as he saw me, Ron's mischievous smile melted into a tender look of concern.

"How'd it go last night?" he asked.

I gave him a slight nod. He instantly understood. In a friendship like ours, sometimes words are unnecessary. We walked through an opening in the chain-link fence and into the large open fields of the school grounds. It was Saturday, and the emptiness of the schoolyard seemed to deepen my despair.

"So, do you want to talk about what happened last night?" he said.

"I'm running away," I said.

He stopped and turned to me, his arms spread out at his sides in a gesture of disbelief and bewilderment. "What do you mean, you're running away? It can't be that bad, can it?" he asked. "Besides, where would you go?"

"Florida."

"Really? Are you serious? You're serious, aren't you?" he asked. "You can't run away! You have no money. No way to get there. Nowhere to stay."

"So! I'll figure it out somehow," I said. "I'm doing it! I'm leaving tomorrow."

"Tomorrow!" He grabbed my arm. "Jay, you can't do that. You'll never make it out there alone."

I stared at him for a moment. "So, you're coming with me then?"

"What? . . . No! . . . I don't know . . . Maybe . . . ," he stammered. "Geez, Jay. We can't."

"Why not? We both suck at school, and because of that, we're always in trouble with our parents. Now my dad is threatening to send me to military school," I said. "Let's just leave this place and go to Florida."

"We can't," Ron insisted.

"I'm going!" I fired back and turned on my heel to leave, anger rising like an iron fist in the pit of my stomach. "I've got to pack while my parents are still out. So, you better meet me here tomorrow morning at eight, or you may never see me again—ever."

I stormed off in the opposite direction, the quick way home, and left Ron standing in the empty field, shaking his head and clenching his fists. Had I turned around, I might have seen him crying.

The entire evening was a blur—my only memory is of lying in bed, anxiously waiting for the next day to come and take me away. But the next morning is as clear as if it happened yesterday:

It is Sunday. All bundled up for winter and wearing a knapsack stuffed with clothing, I walk around the block to the park, confident that Ron will be there, but the park is empty. Nauseous and afraid, I am about to turn back when suddenly from down the road I see the figure of a boy with what looks like a knapsack walking toward me. I know, even from the distance, that it is Ron.

We greet each other with silent nods. Then we sit on a bench in the park that we were practically born in. We're talking, our heads bent slightly toward each other—holy brothers united by a bond that knows no time, as strong and sure as the force of gravity. Ron puts his arm around my shoulders and convinces me to stay. I ask him why, then, did he bring his knapsack. He turns to me, and smiles.

"Just in case I couldn't stop you."

—*Jason Berzow*

Moments in Time

In the nook of a mountain on the edge of Pisgah National Forest in North Carolina, a crumbling old house nestles comfortably in a grove of giant white pines. Its tin roof sags. Its redbrick chimney threatens to collapse. Weathered boards hang free. Hemlocks and ivy hover over a bubbly stream winding lazily around a June-apple tree. The driveway dips and curves, finally resting under a maple tree whose branches stretch over a sprawling rosebush. In one room of the once-white house lives a man as wizened and gnarled as a mountain laurel. His name is Frank.

Frank has been deaf from his birth, more than eighty years now. He cannot speak, although colorful language pours from him like water cascading over boulders—not as formed words, but in hand gestures, actions, expressions, smiles, and eyes that sparkle like dew in sunshine. His back is bent grotesquely and has a large hump. His feet and legs are swollen from heart disease, his breathing labored by emphysema. Only strangers sorrow for him. His friends know the joy he derives from life.

I stand in awe of him, this gentle man who has become my friend. He makes me laugh and cry and continually captures my undying admiration.

We sit one afternoon on stumps in his backyard, the sun blazing down on our heads. As a nearby stream whispers its infinite melody, a cardinal splashes bits of bright red in the treetops. With expressive gestures, Frank is drawing a new picture on the blackboard of my brain. Enthusiasm drives him to his feet to emphasize the story with exaggerated motions.

"Long, long time ago, I built sawmill. Way back. Way back in the woods. In a cove. Mountains all around. Big mountains."

He utters not a word, because he cannot, but sounds emerge from the depths of him, sounds of intense feelings, imprisoned, wanting escape. The bony fingers create falling water and a turning wheel. Nails are placed with invisible tools. Now, a dreamy expression covers his face.

"Had a good stream," he tells me. "Tumbled over huge rocks. A waterfall. Made a waterwheel. Big one. Enough to power my sawmill."

"Worked hard," he demonstrates. "Fine piece of equipment. Sawed boards good. Really good when the rains came and swelled the stream."

I thank Frank for his story and head home. The tale rolls around in my mind. Curious, while visiting his sister who lives across the East Mountain, I ask, "Did Frank actually build a sawmill back in some remote area in the mountains?"

"Indeed, he did," she says. "In the Hanging Dog section

of Cherokee county, about fifty miles from here. Our family used to live there. He carried the mandrel about fourteen miles across those mountains on his back. There were no roads, then, back in the cove."

A mandrel . . . I know a mandrel is a long, steel spindle, the main piece required for construction of a sawmill, also the heaviest. I walk into the woods behind our house to where there are pieces of an old sawmill. The mandrel is eight feet long, my tape measure says, and eight inches around. I try to lift it. I cannot. The magnitude of this task is unbelievable. But then, Frank is always showing that when the desire to achieve is great enough, there are no limits to one's ability.

"Come with me," motions Frank on another lazy summer day. "Show you my workshop."

I follow the bowed figure in ragged work clothes and a grease-stained cap. The worn leather belt gathers folds of trousers now too large for the thinning waist. Inside the slanting shack, its gray boards ragged with age, is the most complete hardware supply imaginable: cans, boxes, and barrels filled with castaway items gathered over the years line the walls, carefully treasured for whatever use he might find for them. Piles of old lawn mowers, tillers, motorcycles, and bicycles snake a crooked line down the center. To the left of the door, a variety of tools, shining and smooth, lean against the wall. On the right stands an old gasoline-powered washing machine.

"First time I've ever seen one of those, Frank."

Watching my lips form the words, he utters, "Ya, ya."

With a big grin, he demonstrates its efficient working process. "Have to carry hot water from the house," he acts out.

"I like your workshop, Frank," I compliment sincerely.

A satisfied smile lights his features. He can read lips and people well.

As we step outside, a plane drones overhead. A gnarled finger points skyward, signaling he has noticed the glint of silver in the sun. Suddenly, Frank has another story to tell. Excitement registers in every fiber of his being. We sit on the ground, surrounded by purple periwinkle blossoms, as he sketches an imaginary picture in sharp detail.

"Many years ago . . ." He flips pages of an invisible calendar backward to show the date. "I built a plane . . . little one. Would fly!" He sails his arms in the air. "Made of wood . . . old boards and packing crates. Had a fine, big motor. Worked a long time on it. One morning, bright, clear, I cranked the engine and climbed in. The plane was clumsy. Bumped along. Did not want to lift off. Then it did! Flew over the cow pasture. Crashed into apple tree . . . yonder." He points to a twisted dead tree trunk across the field. His face falls, "Crumpled, splintered. I was sad. Climbed down." He is smiling again. "Was not hurt." With a flip of his hand and only a backward glance, Frank shows how he walked away with calm resignation, the next project bright in his mind.

How many mechanical marvels has this little man built in his lifetime? How many miles has he cycled around the community until age and infirmities compelled him to give it up? Folks used to bring him broken bikes to fix, and he was happy.

The years pass. Frank grows feeble and is cold even in the stifling heat of summer. He withdraws from most activities, even from working in his shop, except on the warmest of days. One afternoon, I mow for him while he sits on the bank, watching to see that I steer carefully around the purple thistles and sunny field daisies. To him they are the prettiest of flowers. Raspberry bushes grow in utter confusion, bearing gallons of luscious fruit. The prickly bushes grow wild, making mowing almost impossible. He refuses to allow me to prune them back into submission. He picks a few that grow close to the house. With a gesture, he urges me to pick the rest.

The clock in Frank's room slowly ticks away the seconds. He loves clocks almost as much as he loves the engine in his broken lawn tractor. His self-taught knowledge and natural ability have guided him through a lifetime of clock repair. From his sister I had learned of the incredible clock that ran on marble power. Using the waterwheel theory, he cunningly persuaded marbles to drop at an even pace into slots on a tiny wheel. The wheel turned the hands, producing an accurate timepiece. I wondered if he still had it, tucked away in one of the many boxes stacked against the walls.

Staying in his room to keep warm is driving him to boredom. But the chill winds of a departing summer make aging bones ache, and swollen legs make walking excruciating. He sits on the bed. It is his couch during the day. A picture of a red construction crane torn from an old industrial magazine hangs from a tack on the wall. To him, the obsolete machine is a mechanical marvel. His shaggy head shakes with resignation. Hopes and dreams fade into years past. No more . . . no more. The clock ticks on, a sound he cannot hear. Suddenly the faded eyes rest a moment on the clock, then travel to Sunday's *Parade* magazine lying open to the back page. A symphony of stars lights his eyes as he hands the magazine to me. It's funny . . . I now notice how a person's eyes can speak. "This grandfather clock is ready to assemble," the ad reads. "Only $149.95."

Frank produces a frayed wallet, from which he pulls a stack of bills. "Enough?" he questions.

I nod my head. I know it is all he has. His welfare checks are meager.

"Will you get me one?" his actions ask.

"Sure, Frank. We'll go together, you and me, okay?"

At the store, he pulls out the precious bills and places them on the counter.

"The works. Where are the works?" I ask, looking through the boxes.

"They are separate," says the clerk. "That will be another $149.95, plus tax."

My heart breaks as I explain to Frank. I should have read the fine print.

Undaunted, he tucks the boxes under his arms. "Later," he motions. "I can get the works later, when my checks come."

Weeks pass before the money is carefully hoarded and we bring the precious time mechanism home. Immediately, he begins the tedious task of construction, placing the many complicated pieces about the cluttered room. Gradually the cabinet takes shape under a shower of tacking and gluing. Then he assembles the delicate works and mounts them inside. The chains and weights gleam bright gold against the dark walnut wood. Then come the chimes, hauntingly lovely to hear. How Frank loves that clock!

"Can you hear?" he asks with each of my visits. "Is it pretty? Does it go *bong . . . bong . . . bong*? Loud?"

"Yes, Frank, it's the most beautiful clock ever."

Nodding, he sits back contentedly, watching the weights move rhythmically, back and forth, back and forth.

The long winter is again upon us. The grandfather clock is measuring time rapidly for Frank. A twinkle can still be found in his eyes. A smile is always on his face. An insatiable interest in all things still keeps him company. He is eagerly waiting for the blooming of the tiny lavender crocuses planted in a neat row under the rose-bush. He waits for the raspberries, the thistles, the daisies. He waits for the warm sun to come again so that he will feel better.

He must fix the old lawn tractor, he says, to carry him back and forth to the mailbox. And the broken table leg. And the torn screen door.

"I know, Frank. I know you have much to do."

I wait for the greening of the landscape. A late snow falls, covering everything with a heavy icy blanket—it is unusual, this late in March. The old house huddles under its cold, white hat, and the neglected porch timbers tremble with the weight. The bare mountains transform into a winter wonderland, so beautiful that my whole being aches with mysterious longings. Frank would not like it. "Cold . . . too cold," he would say.

I am glad he is no longer here, for I know he is happier in that place where there are no nights of pain and where the wild sweet flowers bloom forever. He is there, I know, for he told me once, with sighs of ecstasy, that he was going there. A restless longing stirs me—it is my yearning to know that now, now he can hear the chimes ring forth from his beloved grandfather clock. You can, Frank. I know you can.

—*Joyce Lance Barnett*

Surprise Party

I was not looking forward to my twelfth birthday. My mother had been gone for almost two years, and my last birthday had come and gone without notice. I knew this birthday would be no different.

I had run out of things to look forward to. For a time, school had been my escape from the emptiness of home, and I excelled at most subjects. But soon I dreaded school as well. There was little about my life that I liked or cared about. The only thing I wanted was a different life—or none at all—or to be Steph Hitz.

Steph Hitz was a bubbly, popular girl in my sixth-grade class. To my eyes, she had everything going for her and everything to look forward to. She lived with both parents and a sister who hardly ever fought with her, in a quaint old stone house with gingerbread trim near the creek. I knew this because I'd walk home from school along Quittapahilla Creek and linger along its edge to look at her home through the twisted trees. To get there, you had to walk across a wooden bridge. Sometimes one of their horses *clop-clopped* across the bridge as if to greet

Steph when she came home from school. Sometimes their shaggy dog scampered to her. An orange cat always trailed behind. Sometimes her mother was in the garden, adding vegetables or flowers to a basket looped over her arm. She always put down the basket as Steph and her little sister ran with outstretched arms toward her. I always had to turn away then, trudging home along the creek, skipping stones or doing whatever I could to prolong returning to my own desolate house.

Just before my twelfth birthday, Steph invited me to her house after school. At first her invitation surprised me, because we didn't talk much at school. But she was everyone's best friend; that's just the way she was. I eagerly accepted her invitation.

Her mother took my book bag and greeted me with a smile. Her kindness brought tears to my eyes. With her arm around my shoulders, she led me into the house. I gasped. The interior looked like one of those Victorian dollhouses I had always wanted. The rooms were filled with antique furniture and freshly cut flowers. The hard-wood floors shone, and I had to resist the urge to slip out of my shoes and slide across them in my stocking feet.

When Steph asked whether I wanted to see her room, I eagerly nodded my head and bounded up the stairs behind her. Again I caught my breath. Her room smelled like flowers, and her four-poster bed was so high you needed a stool to climb on top of it. A handmade quilt was fan folded on the bottom. Lace curtains billowed in front of six-foot windows, and flowered wallpaper covered her walls. Her bright cheerful room stood in sharp contrast with my small room with teeny windows and unpainted walls.

She let me climb on top of her bed, where we played a board game. She had to teach me the rules, because I had never played it—or many other board games—at home. Steph was patient and never made fun of me, even when I made mistakes or forgot the rules.

After a while, Mrs. Hitz poked her head into the room. The smell of chocolate wafted in after her.

"Are you baking?" Steph asked her.

Mrs. Hitz smiled and told Steph her mind was playing tricks on her. Then she winked and closed the door. As we were finishing the game, Mrs. Hitz returned and said it was time to go to the dining room. Figuring it was their dinnertime, I gathered my things to leave. But before I reached the door, Mrs. Hitz steered me into the dining room, where Steph's dad and little sister waited. The table was set with five glasses and five china plates. Around each setting were party favors and foil hats.

"Surprise!" her little sister said, shaking a noisemaker. It wasn't until they all cried "Happy birthday!" that I realized it was all for me.

Mrs. Hitz pulled out a chair and called me the guest of honor. My head spun, my cheeks burned, and my eyes blurred. I choked back tears as they sang "Happy Birthday" and Mrs. Hitz brought out a chocolate layer cake and set it in front of me. The family beamed, and they made a huge production of me cutting the cake. My hands shook, and Steph had to help me put wedges on the plates.

As we ate the wonderfully moist and sweet cake, Mrs. Hitz gave me a package wrapped in pink-and-white striped paper and pink satin ribbon. I blushed again, being too nervous to accept it. "Please open it," she said.

Tears threatened to burst as I unwrapped the paper, careful not to tear it. I had never felt such thick, silky paper. Inside were two tortoiseshell combs. Mrs. Hitz said something about wearing them in my "beautiful long hair." She came to my side of the table and put the combs in my hair as gently as if I were her own daughter. I couldn't hold back my tears. She let me bury my face in her shoulder. "Shh . . ." she whispered and rubbed my back.

Eventually, I pulled myself away. It was growing dark, and I had to make the trek home along the creek. I refused their offer to drive me home. I didn't want them to see where I lived. As I walked, I was unaware of my surroundings. I kept touching the combs, making sure they didn't disappear, as I replayed every detail of my birthday party, trying to imprint it forever in my memory. I wanted to share my happiness with someone, but as usual, the house was empty. It would be that way for many years.

I'd like to say that Steph and I became the best of friends after that day. In truth, we grew no closer, nor more distant. But her smile and the tortoiseshell combs were a source of comfort for many years afterward.

—*Rita Marie Keller*

 Bozo

For a long time after the death of my cat, Bozo, I found it hard to talk about him. I was a little embarrassed and genuinely surprised at how fragile I was on the subject of the old boy's passing. After all, I was a big, tough guy, and he was just a cat. I was also a writer, and so, not surprisingly, I soon found myself reminiscing about him on paper.

It is fitting that I should write about Bozo. He was with me at the very beginning of my writing career. He was there through uncertain jobs at local newspapers and flashier gigs at city magazines. He was there as my freelancing practice grew into more than just a stopgap between jobs. He was there through more than twenty books and half a dozen screenplays. He sat with me on a corner of my various desks as I cobbled together millions of words, many of them published, some still gathering dust on a shelf or buried in computer files—and none of them about him. I guess I owe him a sentence or two after all that.

I first met Bozo in May 1986 at the Toro Park Animal Shelter, just south of Salinas, California, where I was living at the time with my girlfriend, Jennifer. I had been in the Golden State for just under six months, and I had the not-so-bright idea of giving her a kitten for her birthday. (A word to any men reading this with a similar idea: jewelry. To any women: dog.) The animal control officer in charge sent me to the "kitten room," a large cage in which dozens of fist-sized, mewing fur balls swarmed over a vast carpeted jungle gym. They were all achingly cute, and I wanted to take every one of them home. They, however, wanted nothing to do with me. As I stepped into the cage (it was that big), all of them fled to the far corners or skulked inside the jungle gym's many hidey holes.

All but one.

A single, gray-striped kitten stood in the center of the room, alone, looking up at me, looking me right in the eye. He cocked his head to one side, curious but unafraid, and then walked up, put a paw on my shoe, and said, "Meow!" That brash display of courage won my heart, and without a second thought, I picked him up and took him home.

Within a few days, what I'd seen as courage quickly manifested into near suicidal recklessness. No matter how high the counter, no matter how distant the ledge, he tried for it. He leapt and fell, leapt and fell, leapt and fell. He landed on his back, his head, his butt—anywhere but his feet. He dragged things down with him: appliances, dishes, houseplants, a radio. One day, at the sound of yet another crash, I rushed into the kitchen, fed up and fully prepared to test the efficacy of our garbage disposal on young pets. But at the sight of this fierce and determined little kitty cat, sprawled comically on the floor, tangled in a dishtowel and surrounded by cutlery, I just had to laugh. I thought, what a clown!

And so, I named him Bozo.

I decided early on that Bozo would remain indoors. My first wife, Lori, and I had lost a sweet-natured little cat named Roxy back in Iowa City to a merciless pickup truck that left her broken and dying in agony in the street. When I went to the local shelter to look for another kitten a few weeks later, the animal control officers made me fill out a form, read a handful of pamphlets about the benefits of raising cats indoors, and then informed me that there was a waiting period before I could adopt another pet. Despite the officers' warnings—probably because of them—we let Lilly, the kitten who eventually came to live with us, run outside when she grew up. But the message had gotten through to me, and I worried about her. By the time I met Bozo, I was sure that I couldn't stand to see him dead in the street.

Bozo grew quickly into a tall, lean, and handsome cat, mostly gray with dark stripes and apricot undertones. His fur was short and somewhat bristly. His head was tapered and regal, his neck was thick and powerful, and his eyes were a dark hazel-green.

Even as a kitten, he displayed an uncommon intelligence and sensitivity to human moods and signals. But he was never what you'd call a friendly cat, at least where other people were concerned. Me, he loved, and our assorted roommates he tolerated and occasionally tortured, but strangers reached for him at their peril.

I'd always heard that you can't train cats, but then I'd always heard that they land on their feet, so from the beginning of our relationship, I dealt with Bozo as a unique creature. He was less than a year old when I discovered that he would fetch wads of notebook paper that I threw across the room. He soon learned to jump up onto my shoulder from nearly anywhere, including the floor.

He loved to play a run-and-chase game we'd learned from my old friend, Richard, who roomed with us for a while in Salinas after Jenny moved out. Rich called the game Commando Kitty. It went like this: I would hide around a corner, let Bozo see me there, and then make a certain pensive facial expression. Bozo would clamp onto me with a predatory gaze and slink over to the corner, whereupon I would dance away fearfully while he pursued and took swipes at my ankles. When I had nowhere else to run, I would turn, growl, and chase him. When Rich played the game, he added an element of danger: the Savage Knit-Comforter Net of Death. But when Bozo and I played, we just chased each other around the apartment. We sometimes played like this for more than an hour at a stretch.

In Los Altos, where we lived with my second wife, Gina, Bozo and I developed another game. It was a kind of handball played with a hunk of Styrofoam that we bounced off the sliding glass patio doors. I nearly always outscored him, of course, because his claws tended to catch in the "ball." But he beat me once in a while; he had a devastating kill shot.

I never had Bozo declawed, a decision I don't regret one bit, because it's a monstrous practice, the equivalent of cutting off a finger at the first joint. But cohabitating with a large, crabby, fully armed feline is a lot like living with a furry Freddy Krueger. For years, every single piece of furniture I owned was in tatters! Slashed sofas! Lacerated love seats! Ripped rugs! When we moved in with Gina and he began to slice and dice her furniture, my cat became a source of stress in my marriage. I tried everything, from nasty sour-apple sprays to sticky tape, but nothing would dissuade that cat from flaying the furniture. And he would *not* use a scratching post, no matter how well designed. Carpet-covered or rope-wound, freestanding or doorknob-hung, he would have nothing to do with them when a perfectly good couch was available.

I had nearly convinced my wife that life without upholstery was possible and even desirable, when I found something that Bozo actually liked clawing better than our furnishings. It was a clever assemblage of corrugated cardboard called Bizzy-Kitty, and he just loved it. You could almost hear him saying "Ahhhh" as he dug into the thing. To the end of his days, Bozo would use that unmistakable claws-in-cloth sound to summon me (he could wake me from a dead sleep with the faintest pluck of cushion), but for the most part thereafter, he left the furniture alone.

Lively as Bozo was, he never displayed much enthusiasm for the thousands (okay, hundreds) of cat toys I brought home for him over the years. He always preferred wads of paper, clumps of string, and, of course, the sofa cushions. There was one exception: Shortly after Bozo and I moved to Palo Alto, where we lived as bachelors for the last seven years of his life, I picked up a stuffed doll made to resemble Newt Gingrich, then Republican Speaker of the House of Representatives. Illustrated in cartoonish detail, it was laced with catnip. Whenever Gingrich's face appeared on CNN, I would shout, "Bozo! Get Newt! Baaaad Speaker of the House!" And my loyal Demo-cat would pounce on that doll, hug it close with his front paws, and shred it with his back claws. I always felt better when he did that. I think he did, too.

At around age ten, Bozo began gaining weight, and by fifteen, he was waddling. Even with the extra pounds, he remained as lively and clear eyed as ever and was usually still up for a few rounds of Commando Kitty, but I switched him to low-cal cat food anyway. When he began losing weight, I simply thought the new regimen was working. After he had slimmed down a bit, I switched back to his regular food, but his weight kept dropping. He continued to play with my other cat, Bijou, a stray we had collected a few years earlier, and he still loved to fetch wads of paper, but I noticed he was beginning to tire easily. He began spending more and more time sprawled on my lap, dozing. I thought he was just getting old. The vet told me that bringing him in sooner wouldn't have helped, but I think he was just letting me off the hook.

Bozo had been at the Adobe Animal Hospital for a few days when I stopped in to see how he was doing. As I approached his cage, all the white-coated animal docs and their assistants warned me to be careful. They caught a collective breath as I opened the cage door and casually stuck my head inside. Bozo was especially affectionate, purring loudly at the sight and smell of me in an uncharacteristic public display of emotion. He looked better than he had in months. While I was petting and reassuring him, I noticed shreds of white lab coat near the corner where he had been sleeping.

A day later, I got a call from the vet. Bozo's test results were in: His kidneys were permanently damaged and shutting down. He had looked well and strong when I visited, because they were forcing fluids into him intravenously. Without intravenous fluids, he would quickly become sick and miserable, and whatever the treatment, he would be dead within a few months.

My decision to end Bozo's life was astonishingly difficult, and I nearly backed out at the last minute. He had been my constant companion through my entire California adventure. He had been with me through feast and famine, through girlfriends and roommates and wives and blessed solitude. He'd always been there, grumpy and uncompromising, mistrustful of strangers, a lifelong house cat who lusted for the outdoors, even though it terrified him the few times he'd slipped out into the wild and fluttering green. He was my pal, loyal as a dog, full of piss and vinegar, and suddenly I just could not accept responsibility for his death.

A young vet named Hill read the indecision on my face and said, "He's had a good run. He's been happy and healthy all his life. Do you want his last few months to be his worst?" I did not.

Bozo passed away in my arms on July 2, 2001, at 3:11 P.M. As the light in his eyes dimmed and the strength in his body faded, I stroked his head and told him he was a good boy, a very good boy.

And he was.

—*John K. Waters*

My Enemy, My Friend

The first time I saw him, he was pointing a machine gun at us. It was early spring of 1945, and my grandparents and I had just emerged from a bunker, where we had spent a terror-filled night.

I was nine years old and living in Hungary with my grandparents, who were raising me. World War II raged around us, playing havoc with our lives. We had been on the road for many months, traveling in our horse-drawn wagon, searching for a safe place. We'd fled the village of our births in the Bacska region when Tito and his Communist Partisans (guerrillas) began closing in. By day we'd move swiftly, ready to jump out and take cover in a ditch if warplanes approached. By night we camped along the roadside with other refugees. I usually lay bundled up in my feather bed in the back of the wagon, cradling my orange tabby cat, Paprika. War was almost all I had known my whole childhood. There seemed to be no safe place to be found.

After the Christmas of 1944 when we were almost killed in the bombing of the city we were in at the time, Grandfather decided that a rural area would be safer. So we moved to the country in upper Hungary and settled in a small house that had an old cemetery as its neighbor. There, Grandfather, with the help of some distant neighbors, built a bunker in the ground a short distance from the house.

On the eve of that early spring day in 1945, we'd spent the entire night in the bunker. Warplanes buzzed, tanks thundered, and bombs exploded all around throughout that sleepless night. Finally, at daybreak, everything grew deathly still. Grandfather decided it was safe to go back to our house. Cautiously we crept out into the light of early dawn and headed toward the house. The brush crackled under our feet as we walked past the cemetery. The monuments, separated by tall, dry weeds, looked lonely. I shivered, holding Paprika tightly in my arms.

Suddenly there was a rustle in the bushes just ahead. Two men jumped out and pointed machine guns directly at us.

"*Stoi!*" one of the men shouted. Since we were from an area where both Serbian and Hungarian had been spoken, we knew the word meant, "Stop!"

"Russians!" Grandfather whispered. "Stand very still and keep quiet."

But I was already running after my cat. She had leapt out of my arms when the soldier shouted, so I darted between the soldiers and scooped her up. The younger of the two soldiers, tall and dark-haired, approached me. I cringed, holding Paprika against my chest. The soldier reached out and petted her.

"I have a little girl about your age back in Russia, and she has a cat just like this one," he said. Then he gently tugged one of my blond braids. "And she has long braids, too, just like you." I looked up into his kind brown eyes, and my fear vanished. Grandfather and Grandmother sighed with relief.

Well, both soldiers came back to the house with us and shared in our meager breakfast. From them we learned that the Soviet occupation of Hungary was in progress.

In the following months, many atrocities occurred in our area and throughout our country, but because the young Russian soldier had taken a liking to me, we were spared. He came to visit often, bringing little treats along for Paprika and me, and he always talked longingly of his own little girl. I was terrified of the Russians in general, but I loved his visits. Then one day, almost a year later, he had some disturbing news.

"I've been transferred to another area, *malka* ("little one"), so I won't be able to come and visit anymore. But I have a gift for you," he said, taking something out of his pocket. It was a necklace with a beautiful turquoise Russian Orthodox cross on it. He placed it around my neck. "You wear this at all times, *malka*. God will protect you from harm." I hugged him tightly, and then watched him drive away, tears welling in my eyes.

World War II was over, but for the people of Hungary a life of bondage had begun. Many men who had been involved in politics or deemed undesirable were rounded up by the secret police, never to be seen again. Not long after, the knock on the door we dreaded came: They'd come to take away my grandfather. Fortunately, he managed to sneak out a window. Grandfather went into hiding, leaving Grandma and me to survive the best we could. Not long after, my cat died, and life truly seemed unbearable. Sometimes, I would finger the cross the soldier had given me and wonder where he was. Was he back home with his daughter? Did he remember me?

The time passed in a haze of anxiety and depression. Then, in the fall of 1947, a man came to get us in the middle of the night. He would take us to the Austrian border, where we'd be reunited with my grandfather, who had obtained counterfeit papers so we could all cross the border to freedom. We traveled all that night to a place where the ethnic Germans of Hungary were being loaded into transport trucks and expelled from Hungary. When we arrived, a weary-looking man with a thick, scraggly beard and a knit cap pulled low over his forehead was waiting for us.

"Grandpa!" I cried out, rushing into his arms, so happy to see him again. Together, my grandparents and I moved toward the transport truck loaded with dozens of people and got on, fake papers in hand. I knew if we were found out, Grandpa would get hauled off to prison, and worse, he might be executed. I watched as the Russian soldiers drew closer, and I prayed to God to keep us safe.

One of the guards boarded the truck, and I caught my breath. "Grandpa," I whispered. "Look, it's my soldier, Ivan! He is checking this truck." I wanted to jump up and run to him, but Grandpa shushed me. "Maybe he won't recognize us," he whispered, pulling the knit hat further down his forehead.

In minutes, Ivan stood before us. My grandfather handed over our papers without looking up. I leaned closer and put my hand protectively on Grandfather's shoulder as I peered cautiously at Ivan, searching for the old kind sparkle in his eyes. But he was intent upon the papers, his expression grave. I didn't dare breathe. At last he handed the papers back to Grandpa.

"Everything is in order in this vehicle," he finally said. Then, stealing a wink at me, he walked away and got off the truck. Seconds later, the truck began to move forward. I looked over my shoulder and caught his eye. "Thank you," I silently mouthed, lifting the cross hanging around my neck. He nodded discreetly, and then quickly turned away. As we crossed the border to safety, we all said a prayer of thanks to the Lord.

Although we suffered greatly during the war, the memory of a kind soldier who befriended me and turned my fear to faith will always stay with me. He demonstrated to me that friendship and compassion can be found any-where, even in the heart of an enemy.

—*Renie Szilak Burghardt*

 Weezer

Now that I'm a middle-aged woman, I no longer believe in best friends. So many people have been such good friends to me—it seems unfair to single one of them out as best. But when I was in the second grade, there was no doubt who my number one best friend was. It was Weezer.

At that age, likes attract, and even the slightest differences make kids nervous. The more similar two girls appear to be, the more they're going to like one another. In the little South Jersey town where I grew up, girls who dressed alike banded together. Mothers with the time and money sent their daughters off to school in dresses or pretty skirts and blouses, Mary Jane patent leather shoes, and white ankle socks. Even in kindergarten, we noticed that we *looked* alike, and we figured that meant that we must *be* alike. Weezer and I were just a little bit more alike than some of the others.

We both had dark curly hair. Weezer had a Toni home permanent. I had my Daddy's naturally curly hair, although he wore a regularly mowed crew cut, so I only knew his hair had curl potential from looking at his baby pictures.

We both had nicknames. Our parents had given us lovely, old-fashioned names we didn't care to use. Louise and Josephine were Weezer and Joie, no matter what our mothers or teachers insisted on calling us.

And we were both short. When the class lined up according to height, we always stood next to each other. We were assigned neighboring desks at the front of the room, so we'd be able to see the blackboard without having to peer around some tall boy's head.

Weezer and I were placed together so much that it was inevitable that we'd become either bosom buddies or sworn enemies. Of course, Weezer was too nice to have enemies. She was so nice, and I wanted to be as much like her as possible. I wanted a Toni home permanent like hers, even though my hair was already curly all by itself, and I nearly drove my mother nuts asking for one.

Weezer and I first met in kindergarten, but it wasn't until second grade, when we could walk to each other's houses after school, that our friendship truly blossomed. Only small children and certain breeds of dogs are capable of the unquestioning love we had for one another. We held hands and saved our money to buy matching silver friendship rings at Woolworth's. Once a week we'd stop in to look at the ring display, deciding which design we wanted to buy when we had enough money, changing our minds the next week, then changing them back again.

We weren't the only pair of best friends in our class. Kids tended to couple off, in an instinctive buddy system. Woolworth's did a good business in tiny matching silver rings.

By the time we got to high school, we weren't best friends any more. We'd grown up in different directions—we had different interests, different social lives. Though Weezer was still one of the nicest girls I knew, our paths rarely crossed. In our senior year, we ended up sitting next to each other in English class. By that time, I had a secret boyfriend, much older than I was, and I never dated any of the boys at school. I was so alienated I was voted "most individualistic" in my class. Weezer fit right in, and she'd been holding hands with her steady boyfriend for years.

Not long after graduation, she married him. My last youthful memory of my friendship with Weezer is of her wedding, as she stood in the receiving line at the Methodist Church, looking beautiful in her white lace gown and crying her eyes out. I hugged her and tried to get her to tell me why she was crying so hard. It was the worst case of happy tears I'd ever seen.

Then I went my way, and she went hers. For thirty-one years, I didn't know where she was or how she was, I only rarely thought of her, and I never heard from her. One day, out of the blue, I got an e-mail that someone claiming to be a very old friend named Louise was trying to reach me. "Can this be my dear old Louise from school days?" I wrote. She e-mailed me back: "Yes, this is your dear old Louise, from days of old—Girls' Week, Mouseketeers Club, Christmas shopping. I am so happy to have finally found you."

It turned out we had both been living in California, she in Silicon Valley, I in Los Angeles. She was still married to the same sweet guy—thirty-one years, two daughters, and a granddaughter later. I was still single after many failed relationships. She had been a librarian, her husband the chairman of a small software company. I had been a writer and editor.

We promised to stay in touch. Louise and her husband had retired and moved back East, and they were restoring an old inn on the Chesapeake Bay. I wanted to visit, but didn't know when I could. Neither of us got back to our hometown in New Jersey very often. I had no love for the place. Though my mother still lived there, she visited me in California and we traveled together.

When I got the call that Mommy had died suddenly, I hadn't been back in nearly three years. The news was so tragic and so unexpected, I couldn't cry. I preferred to remain numb. If I started to grieve, I would have to admit that my mother was really dead. On the flight to New Jersey, I ordered drinks until I passed out. At the airport, I fell into my sisters' arms. But we were too busy for grief. Now that we were orphans, we had much to do—a funeral to plan, decisions to make about our family home, accountants and lawyers, caterers and funeral directors to contend with.

For the first time in many years, my two sisters and I all stayed in our childhood home, sleeping in the rooms we had abandoned decades ago when we went off to college. Each of our rooms was still decorated the way we had left it—a galloping horse drawn on the wall of one sister's room, butterfly decals plastered all over mine. At the end of the hall loomed the dark cavern of the empty master bedroom, our parents' room, the room where Mommy had died in her bed. My youngest sister kept white candles burning on the night table.

On the morning of the funeral we hurried around the house, plumping cushions, putting things away, signing for deliveries from flower shops, setting the table for guests who would come over after the services at the cemetery. We dressed in black, getting ready. When my father died, eight years before, my mother had walked around those same rooms in a trance. She kept saying, "I just can't believe it. I just can't believe it." Now I understood how she felt.

The limousine arrived to pick up the remains of our family. We had been able to assemble only us three sisters, a cousin, and an aunt. At the funeral home, as I worked my way through a row of folding chairs at the front of the room, I tripped on the carpet, steadied myself on my cousin's arm, then turned to stare at the casket, trying to convince myself that Mommy was really inside that carved wooden box, that the smiling young woman in the portrait resting on an easel beside it was the mother I had lost. My sisters and I played our parts as best we could, dry-eyed but serious, shaking hands with our parents' friends and neighbors, trying to place their faces, saying "Of course we remember you," and "Thank you so much for coming."

Someone called my name, and I turned to find a short woman pushing chairs aside as she came toward me. I struggled to place this particular face among the jumbled jigsaw pieces of memory. "It's Louise," she said.

"Oh, Weezer, Weezer, is it really you?" I threw my arms around her, and finally, I cried. Her hair was no longer dark brown and curly, but gray and straight, cut in a stylish bob. But we were both still short, still seated at the front of the room. I had been feeling so lost and lonely, even with my sisters beside me. They'd had their child-hood friends with them that day. Now I had mine.

For the first time in more than three decades, Weezer and I happened to be back in our hometown at the same time. I felt as though my mother, my original and most faithful best friend, had somehow sent Louise to help me get through the day.

Perhaps my friends mean more to me than they might if I were busy with a family of my own. My best friends, all of them, have taken the place of a husband and kids. I start every day by answering an e-mail from a best friend on the other side of the country. We don't see each other much, but I always know what she's doing and how she's feeling. Another best friend never lets a day pass without phoning to check in and exchange even the most mundane news with me. I have best friends I see every week, and friends I don't see for months, even years. If I'm defeated, if I'm tri-umphant, if I hit the jackpot, or if I get into big trouble, any or all of them will show up. I don't even have to call. And my oldest best friend held my hand in second grade, and when my mother died. Her name is Weezer.

—*Joie Davidow*

A Friend in Deed

It had been a rough night for Nettie Hudspeth, and it looked like it was going to get rougher. A cold December drizzle was chilling her to the bone, and she could tell by the hot flush on her cheeks and the ache in her eyes when she looked left or right that she had a fever. It was a two-mile walk from downtown, where Nettie stood under the blinking Christmas lights, to the hospital emergency room. Nettie was tough and unsparing of herself. But she knew she couldn't walk it, not tonight.

When you're homeless in a small town, your options are limited, and Nettie's lapses into screaming rudeness had foreclosed many of them. People remembered your face, and your fits, and crossed to the other side of the street. Nettie searched passersby for a kindly face but saw only tired ones. A woman hurrying by with bulging department store sacks pressed a dollar into Nettie's hand without speaking, without looking into her face. "Thanks!" Nettie called after her. "Thanks," she muttered again to herself. "Now what?"

Then she saw him: the softest touch in town, a sure

ride and probably good for ten bucks besides. Randy Downing had helped Nettie before, several times. "Excuse me! Can you do me a favor?" she implored. "I'm sick. I've got to see a doctor. Could you please just give me a lift to the hospital?"

Randy frowned and shook his head. "I'm sorry. I've had a long day, ma'am. I'm out of work, and I've been looking all day, and it's late, and . . . well, you don't want to hear all that, but I can't do it tonight, ma'am. I'm sorry."

He'd had no dinner—no lunch, either, for that matter—and he was tired, cold, and discouraged in a way that went through his down jacket worse than the north wind. Randy put his head down and stomped past Nettie and on down the sidewalk in the rain.

He didn't get far. "Oh, hell," he said to himself half a block later as he turned back. When he caught up to Nettie, he said, "Come on. I guess I can drop you off on my way home." Nettie followed him, silent as a pet lamb.

Randy knew what he was in for. Nobody too sick to walk to the ER is going to suddenly feel well enough to walk back. And walk back to what? Nettie's spot under the Third Street Bridge wasn't exactly the ideal place to recuperate. The trouble with a person like Nettie was, once you started to help her, there was no place to quit. It was going to be a long night.

After Nettie checked in with the ER triage attendant, Randy put his last thirty-five cents into a vending machine in the hospital corridor and then slumped down in the low-backed waiting room seat. Why didn't they make these chairs more comfortable? Nobody ever got out of the emergency room fast—three hours, minimum, was his estimate. Seeing Nettie's famished look, he held the peanut M&Ms out to her, but she waved them away, lost in her own fevered thoughts. Randy stared just as bleakly at the blank wall in front of him. He didn't even notice when Nettie was called into the treatment room.

"You can go now," she said as she nudged his arm to get his attention. "You don't have to wait. I'll be fine now."

"Nah, I'll be here when you get out. You'll need a ride back to town," Randy said. He didn't say "back home." He knew there was no such place.

Exhausted, Randy nodded off several times as he waited. The last time, when he lifted his heavy lids, he noticed a man across the aisle smiling at him.

"You don't remember me, do you?" asked the stranger.

Randy shook his head.

"We worked together last year? That construction job out of Auburn?"

"Oh, sure!" Randy smiled. "Good to see you. What're you doing these days?"

"I'm working a big job down in Fremont. We're buried. We'll be there until March, I'm sure. How about you?"

"I don't have anything right now. Just spent all day looking, but . . ." his voice trailed off, and he shook his head again.

"Well, you ought to talk to my boss. We're down four men over there. He's desperate for guys. You could probably start tomorrow morning. Come on, let's call him right now." Fumbling in his pocket for change, the tall young man walked to the pay phone, Randy behind him.

A few minutes later, the two men were shaking hands.

"See you at six-forty-five!" Randy said as the other man picked up his jacket and left the hospital with the woman he'd been waiting for. Randy looked around the waiting room, now suddenly empty. He walked over to the receptionist sitting behind the big round desk, tears glistening in his eyes.

"Ma'am, I've learned something important tonight, and I have to share it with someone. Can I tell you about the amazing thing that just happened to me?"

"Sure," she said, smiling. "I could use a lift tonight."

—*Sharon Elwell*

Drinking Buddies

During the early years of our marriage in the late sixties, my husband, Jim, a college student, enjoyed evenings out with his friends. Once our first child was born (and when, less than three months later, we discovered he was going to have a little brother sooner than we'd planned), Jim and I both stayed at home most nights.

Jim's best friend, Ray, a man I didn't know well, began coming over on Saturday evenings to play chess. I wasn't sure I really liked Ray, who seemed loud, a bit crude, and extremely opinionated. I supplied the sandwiches and chips; Ray brought the beer. Leaving the two guys to watch the baby, I'd climb into bed with a good book and a glass of milk, grateful for my one evening off.

Jim and Ray enjoyed their food, their game, and their rather heated discussions about everything from politics to literature to the existence of life on other planets. I eventually realized that they often debated just for the intellectual stimulation it brought them. It seemed they would choose a topic and then the stance, usually opposing, that each would take. Occasionally, I had to poke my head out to remind them of the sleeping neighbors, not to mention the baby, who I'd see was often asleep in one of their laps. Secretly, I enjoyed listening to them. They were and are two of the smartest men I've ever known.

The case of beer would disappear as Jim, a slightly built man, tried to keep up with his buddy, who should have played halfback for the Patriots. The beer rarely seemed to faze Ray, but Jim, at less than 120 pounds, simply didn't have the same capacity. He usually quit before Ray—usually. Several times I went out to the living room in the wee hours and threw blankets over both of them where they lay.

At one point, Jim developed a severe kidney infection. The doctor prescribed medication and told him "no beer for four months." Instead, he had to drink a quart of cranberry juice a day. What a sentence for a college student.

Jim didn't want word spread around campus about his problem and was going to cancel his chess game with Ray that week. Reminding him that he'd have to cancel every week for four months, I talked him out of it. Between going to school, working, and spending time with his new son and eternally pregnant wife, he didn't get a lot of downtime. I knew how much he looked forward to those evenings. I also knew he'd have difficulty passing up a shared beer with his friend. So I called Ray without telling Jim and explained the situation. He told me not to worry; he'd take care of it.

Saturday arrived, complete with a raging snowstorm. I made spaghetti and meatballs for dinner and purposefully put on a pot of coffee. As the wind howled, we wondered if Ray would make it. The phones were out, so we couldn't call him. Then right on schedule, there he was, clomping up the outside stairs to our second-story apartment, looking like the abominable snowman—complete with the usual case of beer bottles on one shoulder.

I must have looked upset, because he shook his head slightly while Jim took his coat. When I began to say something, Jim gave me "the look" that meant "don't you dare give away my awful secret." Ray sat down at the table and while I dished spaghetti onto his plate, grabbed a bottle from the case, and took a healthy swig. Jim, glaring at me, did the same and nearly choked—on cranberry juice!

Ray then proceeded to give his best buddy a lecture about real friendship. He berated Jim for not trusting him enough to tell him what the situation was and for simply chugging from the beer bottle in defiance of his doctor's orders. Ray asked if Jim valued their friendship so little that he would put himself at risk for stupid pride.

"I don't want to go through life without you, man," Ray said.

That outburst woke up the baby, and before I could get to him, Ray had my son in his arms and was pleading with the little guy to grow up less stubborn than his father. (He didn't.)

For the next few months I supplied the cranberry juice, and Ray brought pizza or fried chicken. Ray absolutely detested the juice, so he began to drink coffee and soda more frequently. I joined them for more of the evening and eventually learned to play chess, though never well enough to satisfy either of them. I was pleased when they began including me in their discussions, and I was delighted when they realized I could hold my own quite well. We talked about all sorts of things, including how we all wanted to travel as far as we could from our little corner of New England.

A few years later, Jim and I left Massachusetts with our three sons. We moved first to Texas, then to Wyoming, on to Washington, and finally California. Ray still lives in the house he inherited from his parents back in the Berkshires of western Massachusetts.

In 1977, I returned alone to Massachusetts for a brief visit. My folks, who had gotten to know Ray through their genealogical club, invited him for dinner one evening. The following night he took me to a club that another friend had just opened. When he brought me home, I kissed him on the cheek and said good-bye for what I knew would be several years. I might note that my father witnessed the kiss and was a bit disconcerted by it. I reassured Dad that there was no problem with either my marriage or my friendship with Ray.

I flew home a few days later, bursting with the news I'd been suspicious of before the trip. As I gave the kids the things I'd brought them, I told Jim I'd brought him something, too, but he couldn't have it for several months. His gift turned out to be our fourth son, Ray.

Jim also made a quick trip back to New England to act as best man when our confirmed bachelor friend was married. They did not see each other again for another fifteen years, but the bond between them has never wavered. The promised frequent visits never occurred, but they've been a constant presence in one another's lives. When Jim's elderly parents needed someone strong to help them from time to time, Ray and his wife, Barbara, were there for them, and they became friends in their own right. In 1998 when Jim's mother passed away, Ray acted as her pall-bearer. When Jim's dad passed away less than a year later, Ray was by our side. That's when he gave Jim the old chess set the two of them had used thirty years before.

Although the times they've spent together have been few and far between, the strength of their friendship is as strong as ever. While both men have put their immoderate drinking days behind them, whenever they meet for a drink, Ray stands the first round. It is always cranberry juice.

—*Marcie Hoye Cumberland*

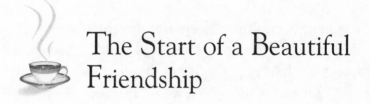

The Start of a Beautiful Friendship

"Can Michelle sleep over tonight? Pleeeease, Mom?" I must have sounded that familiar chant thousands of times while I was growing up.

My best friend, Michelle, and I loved sleepovers and spent countless nights at each other's house from the time we were about five years old until we left home for college in our late teens. Even after she moved to a town thirty miles away during our elementary school years, we remained close by spending weekends during the school year and entire weeks during the summer at one house or the other. Inseparable, we never seemed to tire of one another's company.

All of those wonderful memories of best friends and sleepovers came rushing back to me recently when my oldest son, Jamie, hosted his first overnight friend. Just a week earlier, he'd told me he wasn't quite ready to start sleepovers yet, and I'd assured him that he didn't have to until he felt comfortable. So, imagine my surprise when a pleasant afternoon playing with his friend Danny ended with an until-then unheard, but so familiar, refrain:

"Mommy, can Danny sleep over tonight? Pleeeease?"

The two boys looked at me expectantly, their faces glowing from having so much fun that they didn't want it to end. With memories of my own childhood sleepovers with Michelle dancing through my head, I tried to contain my enthusiasm while I quietly questioned Jamie whether he was really, really ready, given the discussion we'd had the week before.

"Yes! Yes! Yes!" convinced me, and we asked Danny's mom. She said that Danny had gone on his first sleepover the previous week, and together we agreed the boys could sleep at our home that night, after a school picnic both families were attending. The boys' whoops of delight brought back to me that exhilarating feeling I'd felt at having my best friend with me for a whole night.

I think I was as excited as Jamie while we prepared for the picnic and planned the night ahead. My thoughts kept drifting back thirty years to my first sleepover with Michelle and to the many sleepovers that followed. We'd play games for hours, enjoy special snacks, and, of course, stay up late, talking and giggling.

Now, as "The Mom," I was approaching sleepovers from an entirely new perspective, playing an important supporting role but no longer in the center of the excitement. It was my first time hosting a sleepover as a parent, and I wanted to start off on the right foot. My parents had always effortlessly embraced my friends within the circle of our family and made them feel at home. I wanted my sons' friends to feel as welcome and comfortable in our house as my friends had always been in my childhood home.

When we arrived at the school picnic, the boys greeted each other with big bear hugs, as if they hadn't seen each other in weeks. When it was time to leave, Danny's dad handed him his backpack and reminded us to call at any time if things didn't go well and Danny wanted to come home. He needn't have worried.

Despite the late hour, we let the boys have ice cream and watch a video when we got home. My husband and I kept saying to each other, "It's okay, this is a special night." Finally, it was bedtime.

We pulled out the trundle bed in Jamie's room and made it up. This alone was a thrilling event, the first time the trundle had been used, other than when Mom or Dad had slept in it when he was sick. I read the boys a book, turned out the light, and said good night. I could tell Danny was feeling a little apprehensive at that point. I told the boys they could talk quietly for a while longer and left the room.

Immediately, I heard the door click softly behind me and saw the light go back on. I opened the door to see both boys sitting up with their Pokemon cards in their laps. Their faces, which just moments before had shown signs of unease, were now lit up with happiness. Remembering all those late nights with Michelle, I smiled and told them they could keep the light on a little longer. After staying up so late, I was sure they'd sleep in tomorrow.

At 7:30 the next morning, our two-year-old son, Craig, ran into our room and woke me up with, "Where are Jamie and Danny?" The night before, he had been fascinated with the whole sleepover concept and couldn't believe that Jamie's friend was actually going to sleep at our house. I glanced at the clock as I forced myself awake and told him, "Shhhh. Jamie and Danny are still sleeping in Jamie's room." Craig quickly replied, "No, they're not. I checked! Where are Jamie and Danny?"

I got up and tiptoed down the hall with him. Sure enough, the bed and trundle were already empty. Moments later, the older boys came running back up the stairs, already wide awake and laughing. They had risen early and just picked up right where they'd left off the night before. I recalled then, through my early morning daze, that this was one of the greatest things about having a friend stay overnight. The fun didn't end until late at night, and then began again the moment you woke up in the morning, unencumbered by waiting for parents to get up or the delay of fun until morning routines were completed.

Their excitement continued all morning. They went from trading Pokemon cards to building with Legos to playing pirates to creating pictures together on the computer. Through it all, I heard not a single fight or harsh word between them. When it was time to take Danny home so that we could make it to a previous commitment on time, the boys pleaded, "Just a little longer? Please?"

Once again, I fell back in time and remembered Michelle and I spending days on end together, never tiring of each other's company. We'd play Monopoly or Clue for hours or spend an entire day pretending we were grown up and had an apartment together. Recording silly songs and pretend shows with our tape recorders could keep us busy for several days, as we ran around one house or the other, laughing together at our own private jokes.

The warmth and love of our special friendship has remained alive for over thirty years—through long-distance childhood moves, college, marriage, and children of our own. Now, my son was embarking on the same kind of journey, cementing a friendship with special memories of times spent together, which could last a lifetime.

We took Danny home where the boys stood with their arms around each other, grinning like crazy, as I filled in Danny's mom on the highlights of the sleepover. After twenty-four hours spent almost constantly together, they both seemed exhilarated and euphoric, if a little tired. We left with promises of another sleepover, next time at Danny's house. I watched my normally hesitant son agree wholeheartedly to stay at his friend's house sometime soon. As we pulled out of the driveway, I smiled to myself and decided to write to Michelle when I got home. I might even suggest a mommy sleepover.

—*Suzan L. Jackson*

All in the Family

Doris and Amy have been friends for so long, neither recollects when they met. The two Iowa farm girls, now in their early fifties, recall playing together in Sunday school as preschoolers, before starting kindergarten. They've been like sisters ever since, some forty-five years or more, pretty near all their lives.

Not only did they attend the same church and same public school, but they also lived in the same rural neighborhood and rode the same school bus. They played together well and often. In fact, on the very first day of kindergarten, Doris was having such a whale of a good time with Amy that she just went on home with her. Of course, when the bus stopped at her house and her brothers didn't know where she was, her mother had some quick checking to do. Her first call was to Amy's mother.

The girls stayed fast friends, nearly inseparable, throughout their school years. Time away from school usually found them together at one home or another. They were each pretty much a part of one another's families—in good times and bad, like when Doris's dad caught his hand in a corn picker during harvest. Eight-year-old Doris and her two brothers stayed at Amy's house while the two dads and Doris's mom sped off to the hospital.

Music drew the friends even closer. Amy and Doris became two-thirds of the Jaddel Trio. They sang together for all sorts of parties, contests, and school events from third grade until they graduated from high school in 1968.

Both Amy and Doris chose local boys from the class of 1967 as their husbands. That's when their paths took different directions. In 1971, Amy's husband graduated from college and was commissioned into the United States Air Force. The young couple left Iowa for parts unknown, while Doris and her new husband stayed in their hometown. Over the many years of her husband's military career, Amy and her family lived in a variety of locations around the country and overseas: New York, Okinawa, Seattle, Germany, Ohio. Doris and her family settled in a farming community in the area in which they'd grown up. She worked as a cafeteria cook at the high school she'd graduated from; her husband managed a local grain elevator. There was at least one similarity in their adult lives: Amy's two sons were about the same ages as Doris's son and daughter.

Though their lives differed in many ways and distance separated them, the two childhood chums stayed close. Never much for gabbing on the phone, they kept in touch with letters, cards, and personal notes. Visits were usually limited to Amy and her family's once-a-year visits to Iowa. As girls, they'd always hoped their future children would be as close as they were. But the four children spent too little time together to be much more than acquaintances.

Amy's husband's last assignment was at Wright-Patterson Air Force Base in Dayton, Ohio, where he was stationed when he retired as a lieutenant colonel. Today, they still reside nearby. Their son, Aaron, spent a year in college there before enlisting in the U.S. Army.

Meanwhile, Doris's daughter, Angie, earned a full scholarship to the University of Cincinnati Conservatory of Music. After graduating from high school in 1991, she headed off to college in Ohio—650 miles away from home but only an hour from her mother's lifelong friend. Soon, Amy's family became like another family to the young woman, away from home for the first time.

Midway through her daughter's college education, in April 1993, Doris was suddenly widowed at age forty-three. Amy rushed to Iowa to comfort her and stayed on for a while to help Doris through that rocky time.

When Amy's son, Aaron, finished his army enlistment, he returned to college and his parents' home in Ohio. He became close friends with Angie, who was still nearby at the music conservatory. And then . . . they began to date.

Their mothers said to one another, "Now, isn't this something?" But they agreed that no matter what happened between Angie and Aaron, it would not cause a problem between them.

Of course, Doris was touched—and thrilled—when Aaron called from Ohio to ask permission to marry her daughter before he proposed. And Amy admits to being pretty excited when the couple announced their engagement.

The two old friends had a wonderful time helping to plan

the wedding of their children. Angie and Aaron were united in marriage at a joyous, musical celebration on a beautiful autumn day in Iowa. Their mothers sang a song together for the newlyweds at the start of the ceremony, while they still could, before their emotions caught their voices.

Later, the mother of the bride smiled softly at the mother of the groom. "This is cool," Doris said to her dearest friend. "Now, we're official."

"Yep," Amy said, clasping her truest friend's hand. "Now we're officially family."

—Billie J. Shelton

My Gardenia Angel

Miss Brown, her dull brown hair pulled into a bun at the nape of her neck and wearing no makeup whatsoever, looked every bit the stereotypical classic schoolmarm. She usually wore soft wool cardigans and shapeless skirts or loose-belted dresses of blue or brown. To my thirteen-year-old mind, my eighth-grade teacher, who was then perhaps in her mid- to late thirties, seemed old. Unmarried, she lived with her truly elderly parents on the other side of town. She drove an old blue Ford and spoke in a gravelly, pedantic monotone. She was both my home-room teacher and my Latin teacher. And I adored her.

She probably took a special interest in me because I was one of her few, if not the only, students who chose to take Latin simply because I wanted to learn it. Certainly adding to my distinction as a pupil was that I was a bright-eyed, good-citizen type who had just enough spirit to attract notice and an eager drive to learn that every teacher dreams of.

After class on my last day of eighth grade, Miss Brown asked about my plans for that summer.

"I'm going to New York for an eye operation," I told her. "They're going to straighten them."

The strange pull of my smile must have revealed the ice-cold terror that ran through my hot, hopeful anticipation. She asked me which hospital. Flattered at her wanting to send me a card, I babbled on that even though my eyes would be bandaged for a week, I was sure someone would read me my mail. No, I replied to her next question, my mother couldn't stay with me. Right after my surgery, she had to return home to go to work.

The doctor my mother worked for in our Pennsylvania town had arranged for my surgery with the eminent chief of ophthalmology at the prestigious Manhattan Eye, Ear, and Throat Hospital. It was my first time away from home by myself. Certainly, I'd never gone to summer camp (though I had one rich friend who had and told me all about it). That year, the twelfth-floor ward of the hospital was to be my summer camp—and the initiation was not into the world of hiking, swimming, and horseback riding, but into the world of surgery.

On the hot, airless June night before my operation, my mother and I took the train to New York City and stayed in a YWCA near the hospital. First thing the next morning, we took the subway to the clinic, where we waited on hard mahogany benches until a clerk called my name.

After surgery, as I emerged from the ether, I felt my mother gently stroking my hair away from the eye mask covering the bandages. When I was fully awake, she held my hand and told me the operation had gone well and she had to leave to catch the train home to Pennsylvania.

A while later, one of the starchily efficient nurses, who, in my newly sightless state, sounded nice and felt young, led me by the hand to the bathroom. As we walked, she described the route and instructed me to feel the walls, memorize my steps, and do whatever else I could to chart my path. My memory of that experience is of a pressing enclosure of black walls with just enough space to move from point to point. It was as if I'd been kinetically transported into the realm of the blind.

After a few days I became quite expert at navigating between my bed and the anteroom where all twelve of us ward mates took our meals together, family style; the tiny balcony where we sat when the sun moved to the other side of the street; the toilets out beyond the ward; and the bathtub room, where I learned to do all my grooming by touch. On about the third day, as I lay in bed for the after-lunch rest and fingered the black eye mask that held no element of Halloween, I heard a rustle beside me. A gentle hand covered mine.

"Hello there," said a gravelly voice, displaced in the alien setting but familiar nonetheless.

Miss Brown had come to New York to attend the World's Fair, she said. "But mainly," she went on, "I came to see you."

Then she placed my hands on either side of a round celluloid box. "Here," she said, moving my hands to the edges of the lid. "Open it."

I pulled off the top and was immediately swathed in the most exquisitely sweet fragrance imaginable.

"It's a gardenia," she explained. "It's creamy white with

large, round, waxy petals. It was the nicest-smelling flower in the whole shop. I hope it lasts till your bandages come off."

She had brought me another gift, from the Holland pavilion of the World's Fair: the teeniest pair of bright blue mittens with yellow trim—our school's colors—linked together by a fine chain of yellow yarn.

"You can pin it on a blouse or sweater," she said, as she guided my fingers over the soft miniatures.

Ninth grade was also part of junior high, so after school started in the fall, I'd often drop by Miss Brown's classroom for brief after-school visits. So began my transition from teacher's pet to teacher's friend. That is when I learned about her hobby of collecting angels and of her ongoing search for unusual ones for her Christmas tree. That Christmas, I scoured the local shops until I found a special one, an exquisite angel with a beautiful face and silk wings, made in France and exchanged for weeks of baby-sitting money. As the saleswoman wrapped it, I felt as thrilled as if I'd just purchased a special item for a cherished collection of my own.

Miss Brown invited me to her home to see it. A look of contained but resonant appreciation lit her soft smile as she pointed it out on the tree. To me it held a lambent radiance, hanging there among the dazzling array of her winged treasures, and the whole gave off a palpable glow in the tastefully traditional living room of the shabby little house. Her mother and her father, a retired Army colonel, entertained me with tea, Christmas cookies, and polite conversation.

When she drove me home, she gave me a beautifully wrapped black box containing a small, blue five-year diary. Its leather cover was stamped with a gold design, and it had a tiny gold lock and key. I wrote in it faithfully, one year in some hieroglyphic code I'd devised. I still have it, intact in its worn-at-the-edges box.

Not until I began writing this story, some five decades later, did I wonder whether she'd had as much difficulty as I'd had with the transition in our relationship—from teacher and student to friends. At bottom, we were both tangling with the same problem, but coming at it from opposite ends.

Once I entered high school, we progressed to the next stage of our friendship, no longer bound by teacher-student strictures of time and place. My biggest hurdle was in calling her by her first name. Only those who grew up in the 1930s or 1940s, or earlier, can relate to the enormity of that challenge. I managed to pretty much skirt the problem during our regular protracted phone conversations, our principal contact those next years.

Throughout my teens, she remained my trusted mentor/friend—observing my progress, cheering me on, and taking obvious pleasure in my emergence from adolescence to early adulthood. I eventually felt more comfortable with calling her Rachel. But I always thought of her as Miss Brown, even after she got married.

Her husband was considerably older, a widower with grown children. She moved down South to live in his family home; by then I'd settled in New York City. I never met him, but the quality of their love and devotion surfaced through the discreet words in her occasional letters. My letters kept her informed of my milestones: my career, my engagement, my marriage, my children. Her response to the first birth announcement was a hand-knit pair of miniature snow-white mittens, cable-stitched down the center and filled with sachet, meant for a drawer or hanger.

In time our contact ebbed to annual Christmas cards. Hers always bore yet another magnificent angel as well as the fondly rendered and as fondly recognized signature. Mine were always filled with highlights of the year's news.

The child-rearing hiatus in my career that followed my second book made the publication of my third, a young-adult novel, an especially significant event. Although dense blocks of time often distanced us, I'd never failed to inform her of the markers in my life. So, as I'd done with my two earlier novels, I sent Miss Brown an inscribed copy of the book, along with an invitation to a local author celebration being hosted in my honor by a nearby bookstore.

As I was preparing to leave for the party, the doorbell rang, and when I answered it, a delivery man handed me a small florist's box. Inside lay a white, fragrant corsage and a card that read:

Because you love gardenias. Congratulations and love, Rachel.

—Corinne Gerson

The Tiger and
the Butterfly

"Mom has had a heart attack," Debbie said. Her voice, though grave, sounded calm over the phone. Debbie's mother, my lifelong friend Barbara, suffered from renal failure, brought on by a long battle with diabetes. The kidney failure, in turn, had caused congestive heart failure. Now she needed heart surgery. This was serious business, but I didn't allow myself to panic. After all, Barbara had fought her way back from perilous illness before.

"Surgery is scheduled for the day after tomorrow," my friend's daughter said.

"I'm coming," I responded without hesitation, mentally rearranging my schedule. Early the next morning, I made the one hundred-mile trek from my home in College Station, Texas, to the hospital in Houston. It was the first of many visits.

I don't know what I expected when I walked into the hospital room that morning, but I was happy and surprised to see Barbara sitting up in bed, engrossed in a daytime soap opera. She was smiling, had good color, and looked great, except for her hair. Usually short, curly, and bouncy, it was greasy-looking and plastered down, the result of a recently missed hair appointment.

"What are you doing here?" she greeted me, as if her hospitalization was no big deal.

"What's wrong with your hair?" I countered.

Then we both burst out laughing. Laughter was one of many things we did often and well together.

After catching up on each other's families, Barbara began to tell me about the "cardiac event," as if it were a humorous episode, rather than the serious situation it was. "When I fell to the floor, I spilled a glass of water and got soaking wet. So I took off my gown, but then I couldn't stand, so I crawled to the bed—buck naked!" Barbara, a short, heavyset woman, knew the visual would make me laugh. And it did.

We reminisced some about good times shared, but mostly we made plans. She was coming to my house for our annual Christmas celebration. We'd already arranged for her dialysis at a clinic near my home. We also planned a short trip to see my daughter's new home in Fort Worth.

"Are you scared?" I asked just before I left to return home.

"Nope. I don't have any control over this, so I won't worry about it."

The surgery went fine, the doctor told us. She didn't look so fine to me. I had never seen so many tubes and wires and machines attached to one person. However, assured that all had gone well, I went home that evening. In no way was I prepared for another phone call from

Debbie. This time her voice was not so steady. In fact, it shook with fear.

"Mom has had a second heart attack."

During my frantic drive back to Houston that night, I prayed over and over again, "God, please don't let her die, please don't let her die." Tears streamed down my face, and I thought about how she would chastise me for crying, remembering the time in high school when the two of us were called to the principal's office. As we walked through the school's corridors to face our fate, I complained, "See what you've done? Now we're in big trouble."

"She's just going to chew us out. It's no big deal. Whatever you do, don't cry. Don't you dare cry!" Barbara fixed me with her look that meant business.

"I won't," I promised.

The principal shook her head sadly. Turning first to Barbara, she said, "Barbara Jean, I might have expected this of you." Then fixing her gaze on me she said, "But Nancy Ray, I'm surprised at you."

I promptly burst into tears. Barbara rolled her eyes, her only sign of frustration at having to put up with a crybaby.

The memory made me smile through my tears, but it did nothing to loosen the knot in my stomach. I nearly jumped out of my skin when my cell phone rang. Not trusting myself to drive and hear the news I feared was forthcoming, I pulled over and took a deep breath before answering.

"She's stable," Debbie said, relief and worry registering equally in her voice. I let out a long sigh and rested my head on the steering wheel.

"They had to shock her three times," she whispered, and my heart froze.

When I stormed into the intensive care unit, the nurse stopped me to ask if I was family.

"Friends for nearly sixty years," I snapped, the don't-give-me-any-flack look on my face making my intentions clear.

"That's family," was all she said.

Barbara was awake.

"Don't you dare bail on me," I said, my tears splashing on her as I bent down to hug her. "And don't fuss at me for crying. You're scaring the devil out of me."

She couldn't talk because of the tube in her throat, but she shook her head slightly, rolled her eyes, and smiled, letting me know there was no hope for her emotional friend. She mouthed, "I love you," squeezed my hand, and seemed to drift off. Exhausted, I laid my head on the bed rail, silently praying, pleading for her life. When I raised my head a little later, Barbara was looking directly at me.

"You tired?" she mouthed.

"You're darn right I'm tired," I said, feigning belligerence.

"Go home," she mouthed once again.

"You tryin' to tell me what to do?"

She closed her eyes and shook her head, conveying that it was futile to try and tell me what to do.

I sat with my friend all that night and began twice-weekly journeys to Houston to visit her. Sometimes, she was conscious and knew me, other times she was somewhere deep within herself. I jokingly complained to her that it was very hard to carry on a one-sided conversation, and I took to reminiscing aloud to her.

Do you remember when we were camping at the beach and took a walk in the tall grass behind the sand dunes and came upon a snake coiled on the path? I froze, and you tried to run, succeeding only in climbing up my back. Now, that's a sight for you: a tall, skinny girl carrying a short, chunky one on her back while the short, chunky one is beating on the tall, skinny one and yelling, "Run, run!"

I relived the myriad trips we had taken together. I talked about our kids and how they'd always had two moms. I recalled how we'd always been there for each other and how we knew everything about each other.

We've talked every problem through, haven't we? Your dad used to fuss at us for talking on the phone so much. There was that time he made us get off the phone, and you convinced me to drive over to your house to finish our conversation, even though my parents had forbidden me to drive the car while they were out of town. It stalled at the stop sign, remember?

So it went for many long weeks, some days better than others. Sometimes the doctors were hopeful, other times somber. Through it all, Barbara's sense of humor prevailed.

One time, she didn't want me to go home. When I tried to leave, she'd mouth, "Don't go." So I'd hang around a little longer. Finally, when a technician came for a procedure, I just slipped out, thinking she wouldn't notice. She did. When Debbie explained that it was late and I had a long drive, Barbara said something like, "I'm going to slap the spit out of her." I laughed when Debbie told me. It was that spunk that made me think my friend would pull through.

She didn't. One cold November morning, a third heart attack took away my forever friend. Debbie's phone calls, the first to announce they were doing CPR, the second to say she didn't make it, left me with an emptiness so vast I thought I would be lost in it forever. When I reached the hospital, Debbie and I stood beside the shell of my friend, her mom, holding each other. For what seemed like a very long time, there were no words. Then, in a tiny voice, Debbie said, "Adopt me, Aunt Nancy."

"You're mine, sweetie," I murmured, smoothing her hair and wondering who on earth would adopt me.

This can't be real, I kept saying to myself that first day. The second morning, I realized with crushing certainty that it was real.

I helped pick out the clothes Barbara was to be buried in; made a collage of pictures of her children, grandchildren, and her; and spoke at her wake about the footprints a true friend leaves on your heart. Driving home after the funeral, I marveled at how two such different people could be such good friends for so long. I was quiet, serious, and sensitive. Barbara was tough, funny, and mischievous. She taught me how to have fun. I think I taught her it was okay to cry. I know that at least once, at the hospital, a tear rolled down her face when I told her I loved her. I wondered how I would get through our traditional Christmas celebration, just a few weeks away. Then I wondered how Debbie would get through Christmas.

Debbie said yes even before I got the invitation out of my mouth. Suddenly, what had seemed insurmountable became doable. There were stockings to personalize, gifts to buy, favorite dishes to make. In doing it for Debbie, I was also doing it for Barbara. In spite of my emptiness, I found myself excited about the preparations and happy to be reaching out.

That Christmas celebration was an especially joyful one. Perhaps Barbara's death made us treasure family and friendship all the more. Having Debbie and her family with my family added so much to our gathering. I loved all the laugher that filled my home, and whenever there was laughter, I felt Barbara's spirit was with us. Though it was a bittersweet Christmas with Barbara gone, it was exactly as she would have had it. The chorus to the song we sang that day seemed to sum it up: "And they'll know we are family by our love, by our love."

Recently, I bought a picture frame with *Friends* written on it. I put a picture of Barbara and me in it, taken when we went to Mardi Gras the year before. I like it because it reminds me to celebrate life, to laugh often. It stands beside a statue of a tiger with a butterfly on his nose that I gave to Barbara years ago when she was collecting tigers. It symbolizes our friendship. If I was an artist, I would have sculpted the tiger in all his regal majesty—and Barbara would have come along and stuck a butterfly on his nose.

—*Nancy Baker*

One Kid at a Time

I was in the army eighteen months, three days, and almost ten minutes. I went in kicking and screaming. I came out just screaming. My mother, Madear, managed to keep the devastating news of my draft notice a secret until after I had joyfully marched across the stage to receive my bachelor's degree. It was, after all, a historic day in our family. The son of a former sharecropper, I had grown up in a three-room shotgun house with no inside plumbing. I was the first in my family to finish college and had already lined up a teaching job on the West Coast. Instead of heading off to a classroom in California, just twelve days after graduation, I was forced to continue my education first at Fort Polk and then at Fort Lewis. There, the U.S. Army taught me to be a killer. I must have been a fairly good student, because I eventually made it out of Vietnam alive.

I missed two planes before the threat of Leavenworth Prison forced me to board the next one out. I landed at Cam Ranh Bay on January 12, 1971. Seven days later, I found myself in Kwang Tree, the demilitarized zone near

Hanoi. My new occupation fresh out of Grambling State University was that of a grunt assigned to the 101st Airborne Division 1st of the 327th AirMobile Unit. My job description was to go into the jungle, search out the enemy, and destroy him.

On one of our missions, we followed a trail up a hill, setting mines on the path behind us. That night as we tried to sleep, we heard the traps go off. The next morning we confidently inched our way down toward the trail to tally the body count. Suddenly, shots rang out. We were in the middle of an ambush. First the lieutenant caught fire, then the radioman. I was next in line. I dove and rolled down the hill, tearing up my leg as a bullet grazed my helmet. I thanked God for the steel pot on my head. Three of our men were hit, one paralyzed.

The injured, including me, were sent back to the base camp, Eagle. That was where I met Lou. Lou was the one real friend I had in Vietnam, and he was probably the best friend I've ever had. Friendships in Nam were hard to form. People were always dying on you. With Lou and me, it was different. We were like brothers. I don't know what made us such good friends.

Maybe we were so tight because he reminded me of my childhood friend, Rabbit. Just like ole Rabbit, Lou always had your back. If someone started messing with you, he had to answer to both of you. Maybe it was because, in a place filled with evil, destruction, and suspicion, Lou was one guy I could trust, and he trusted me.

Lou and I kept an eye out for each other and after somehow surviving each day in hell, we'd lie awake at night on the side of a hill in the middle of the jungle and talk. We'd rap about the crazy war and making it out alive. We'd profess our fears and hopes. We dreamed of starting a black newspaper together when we got home—about saving the world, one word at a time.

When I'd healed enough in the army's eyes, it was back to the jungle for me. There I saw more action, more carnage, more death.

A year in-country was all anyone could take. When my year drew to an end, I was transferred to Fire Base Maude. Lou had also ended up there, and we became hooch mates. We pulled guard duty together, watching to make sure Charlie didn't get through the wire encasing the perimeter. I was there when he got a "Dear John" letter from his wife. He talked about his young son, and I talked about a daughter I had never held, born while I was in Vietnam. And we talked about what it was like, being part of that godforsaken war.

"Bro, Priest, are you scared?" Lou whispered once as we watched the sky light up with military fire.

"Yeah man," I whispered back, "real scared."

Seemed to me that anyone with any sense was scared to death to be there. Those who weren't scared had already gone crazy.

As our time in Nam grew short, we started counting: Three days and a wake-up. Two days and a wake-up. One day and a wake-up. Then, only a wake-up on the day we could leave the firebase and return to base camp and then home. One chopper came in, and Lou insisted I get on. It was the way it should be, he said. I'd seen more action;

it was only right that I leave the hill first. He would catch the next one. I gave Lou the knife that had always hung from my side and told him to hold on to it 'til he got to the rear. I climbed in next to the door gunner and watched Lou standing there, growing smaller as we flew away.

Fog rolled in, delaying the other choppers. There would be no more pickups that day. Later I learned that Lou caught the next chopper out. It was shot down. The chopper and its human cargo burned into the side of a mountain. Lou, my best friend, the guy who was going to help me save the world, was dead.

So when I got out of that hellhole, I screamed. I screamed by roaming the streets at night. I screamed by driving fast cars and running with fast people. I screamed out in pain by talking about Vietnam and Lou until finally, out of desperation, my family cried, "Quit talking about the war! It's over!"

But it would never be over, because Lou was dead, gone in one huge explosion, because he'd let his buddy go first. My family didn't understand why I stayed up all night. They didn't understand that if I stopped moving, I'd have to think, and I'd remember. They didn't understand that sleep was also my enemy, because then I would dream. So I'd stay awake for days until, exhausted, I'd fall asleep on Madear's couch, still dressed in army fatigues, still wearing my boonie hat. Madear would tiptoe quietly around me, thankful that I had found some peace, if only for a few hours. I became a different kind of soldier, fighting battles within my soul. The new enemy territory was an unfriendly civilian world. And I didn't think I would make it out of that war alive. Maybe I didn't really want to.

The guilt of Lou's death hammered at me night and day. It wasn't fair that I had survived and he hadn't. I was supposed to watch his back, and I had failed him by letting him wait for the next chopper, by letting him die. If he had gone first, ahead of me, he would still be alive. The weight of that terrible burden overwhelmed me. It could have kept me down, could have driven me crazy, could have killed me. For many months, all I wanted was to forget, whatever that took, including my death.

Then one afternoon, no different from any of the others, I awoke still groggy from a night on the town and looked in the mirror. A stranger with hollow, hopeless eyes stared back at me.

"Why am I living this way?" I wondered aloud. "Do I fear death and want to live? Or do I fear life and want to die?"

"Maybe," I thought upon further reflection, "I'm afraid of both, of living and dying."

Yet somewhere deep inside I knew I couldn't quit. Quitting would be betraying Lou. It would dishonor him. We'd made too many plans. We'd made a pact to save the world together. But first I had to save myself.

I made peace with Lou that day, and I began my inside-out transformation from warrior to healer. I cleaned myself up and went to the Rapides Parish School Board, where I applied for a position as a substitute teacher. The next fall I was hired to teach fulltime at Jones Street Junior High School, my alma mater. There, I worked with the children most in need, the special education students.

Because of Lou—because he taught me to trust in him and in myself, because he believed in me and in being a positive force for change, and because he taught me the true meaning of friendship—I can now count many blessings in my life. My daughter, born to me during the war, is now in medical school. I live with my wife of twenty-seven years on a farm surrounded by the beauty of nature. I have a loving, supportive family and many good friends.

Since 1986, I have been the principal of the first diploma-bound alternative high school in Louisiana, offering hope to hundreds of young people, of all colors and from all lifestyles, who were once without hope. Some of my students have been runaways, others throwaways. Some have been dropouts and others drug addicts.

My life has been full and rewarding, but none of these riches are mine alone. My best friend, Archie Lucy, sits with me every day in everything I do.

So, I would like to say thank you, Lou, for being my friend. Thank you for making war almost bearable. Thank you for sharing your hopes and dreams with me, and for listening to mine. I miss you. And though I couldn't save your life, I did keep our dream alive. I'm still trying to save the world, Lou, one child at a time.

—*Pat Friedrich, as told by Leroy Priest Helire*

Inner Vision

My daughter, Karen, has a rare eye disorder, a hereditary syndrome for which there is no cure. Her problem is not immediately apparent, and at first sight, you might not realize she has this syndrome. But it still causes her quite a bit of difficulty. Beyond the physical challenges are those not visible to the human eye. Because of her medical condition, Karen is different from other children, and in grade school, nothing is worse than being different. Yet, despite this difference, my daughter has many friends.

During the summer of her fifth-grade year, Karen's retina detached. Fortunately, the problem was caught early enough that it could be repaired with surgery. The operation is an intensely painful one, especially for a child, and requires a very long recovery. As if that were not bad enough, the detached lens could not be reinserted, as hoped, due to complications, and was removed. That robbed Karen of her ability to focus that eye and left her without the natural protection from the sun's harmful rays that the lens provided. During the four-hour ordeal, another complication was discovered: The retina in her other eye had begun to detach. So, the doctors performed corrective laser surgery on that eye at the last minute.

In the days immediately following her surgery, both of

my daughter's eyes were swollen shut and her face was swathed in bandages. She was trapped in a world of darkness and pain, fearful that when she was finally able to open her eyes, she would still see nothing at all.

To take her mind off of the pain, I read to her or she listened to audiobooks. She also called her friends on the phone to talk for short periods of time. Some of her friends professed sympathy as they chatted with her, but were eager to end their conversations with her and get back to enjoying the fun of summer. Others promised to come visit her but never did. Soon, she stopped calling those friends. Karen was very hurt and couldn't understand this treatment by her friends.

There was one exception, one shining example of a true friend that emerged from this experience: Jenny. Before we had even settled in after returning home from the hospital, Jenny visited Karen, bringing her a bouquet of flowers and a small stuffed animal for her "to hug when it hurt." When she realized that Karen could not see her, Jenny quietly slipped up on the bed beside my daughter and took her hand in a gentle grasp, so Karen would know she was there.

Because she was in so much pain, Karen said very little during their visit. She just sat there holding Jenny's hand. The two girls remained there, in virtual silence, for quite a while before it was time for Jenny to leave. She said she'd be back. As I watched her go, I wondered silently if she would keep her promise to visit Karen again.

I vowed that, if she didn't return, I would understand. I knew that the experience had been painful for her as well. As Jenny had sat there in the tomblike quiet of the bedroom with my daughter, I had glimpsed tears of sympathy glistening in her eyes. No, I couldn't blame Jenny if she didn't return. Children's summers are supposed to be filled with fun and games, adventure and freedom. I couldn't fault Jenny if she didn't want to sit in a sickroom with Karen.

But Jenny did return, again and again through the long months of Karen's recovery. She visited after Karen's eye patch was removed, when the light seemed so bright that it hurt to venture outside. She visited when Karen was still unable to ride her bike, or run, or play. She visited regularly in the weeks of constant doctor's visits, when Karen was being fitted for a special contact lens that would protect her eye from harmful UV rays. All through that long, painful summer, Jenny came to see Karen—each time lifting her spirits and making her smile when there was very little to smile about. She nudged Karen into high spirits more times than I can count.

Jenny continued to visit and support Karen into the next school year. She was always there to lend a helping hand and a happy smile, and to defend Karen when others taunted her for being different. Even now, years later, the girls remain close friends. To my delight, Jenny is still a frequent visitor in our home.

I believe that the truest friend anyone can have is the one found in elementary school—that best friend to share the joys and agonies of growing up with, that one other child who sees how things are around you and inside you, then and now, and in between. My daughter, Karen, has such a friend—a little girl whose compassion and kindness have forever touched my heart.

I do believe that Jenny may very well turn out to be the best friend that Karen ever has.

—Jae Worth

☕ Rainy Day Friendship

In the spring of 1997, I traded the hustle and bustle of New York for three months of simplicity and tranquility in a small village in northern Israel, nestled on a hilltop in the lower mountains of Galilee. The village was home to the Ring of Turquoise, a group of storytellers of local renown. An aspiring storyteller myself, I asked to join the group, at least for the duration of my visit. They welcomed me into their meetings and work sessions, conducted them in English on my behalf, and made me feel like I was one of their own.

The two leading members, a couple named Rami and Ifat, were especially warm and gracious to me. Rami is a striking gentleman with eyes at once piercing and gentle. Towering well over six feet, he has a manner of spinning tales that transfixes listeners, carrying them away to lands unknown and times long forgotten. Ifat, his perfect foil, stands slightly more than five feet tall. An untamed halo of soft brown hair surrounds a strongly defined face, punctuated with a jutting chin declaring a determination that her elfin smile belies. With her fleet-footed walk, she is suddenly here then gone, appearing and vanishing like the wind.

Ifat folded me under her wing, and soon I was a frequent guest in their home, where we'd tell stories and
engage in grand discussions on important life matters. On
one such visit, they invited me to stay in their home
during the twelve days they would be traveling in England. My residence at that time was the village's official
guest quarters, a nice-enough, but Spartan, single room
with a hot plate and a teakettle. I was completely floored
by Ifat and Rami's trust and kindness, and though I
secretly doubted my worthiness, I grasped at the opportunity to spend nearly two weeks in their comfortable home.

A few days later, they left amid a flurry of activity and
a few brief instructions. Within no time, I settled in and
happily made full use of the kitchen, cable television,
stereo, and other amenities. It was paradise, and I basked
like a queen in the glow of my new castle.

Several days before my friends' expected return, I went
on a furious cleaning spree, standing on the kitchen
counter to reach the tops of cabinets and scrabbling into
nooks and crannies to exorcise dirt that had been hidden
from view and reach. It was a thank-you gift to my hosts,
I thought to myself, returning to a house that sparkled and
shone even more than it had before their trip. After
proudly surveying the shining results of my hard work, I
took a hot shower and left for the evening.

I returned at 2:00 A.M., happy but tired and in dire
need of a shower after hours of socializing and dancing in
the early Mediterranean summer. As I prepared to bathe,
I noticed that the water heater switch was glowing a fiery

red and was still in its upright position. Only then did I recall the only words of caution my hosts had given me: Never leave the boiler switch on for more than fifteen minutes. It had been on for six to eight hours. I quickly switched it off, mentally kicking myself for being so careless. I went into the bathroom and hesitated for maybe a millisecond before reaching out to turn on the hot water knob on the shower.

A moment of silence was followed by a sound I shall hear in my dreams for the rest of my days. It began as a rattling and coughing as water coursed through pipes unbearably hot and unable to withstand the pressure. The rattling was immediately accompanied by a loud hissing and a thundering that seemed to come from every corner of the house and above my head all at once. Then came the water—dripping from the ceiling and down the walls, creating fissures where there had been cracks and cracks where there had been flawless surface, seeping into paintings hung on drywall that quickly became very wet wall. It rained inside the house—in the kitchen, the salon, the hallway—first drizzling, then pouring onto the furniture, the television, the stereo, saturating furniture and rugs, turning papers and books into soggy clumps.

I dashed around the house in utter panic, suppressing the desire to break down or sob or scream, trying to move furniture and electrical equipment and important papers to dry spots, only to move them again moments later as those spots suddenly became tropical. Then . . . the power went out, the house went dark, and the rains continued, growing heavier still. Then . . . the ceiling caved in. Then

. . . the woman I called for help slipped and fell as she ran up to the house, breaking her arm.

The following morning I made the dreaded telephone call to England, interrupting my hosts' lovely vacation to tell them I had demolished their house. They took the news quietly and with no fuss, giving me the names of whom to call for repairs and saying they would return on schedule the following week. Until then, I insistently stayed at the broken house, perhaps out of some need for self-punishment.

Upon their return to their fallen castle, Ifat and Rami surveyed the damage and set about rebuilding. They directed no recrimination, no blame, and no anger toward me. Their only comment, spoken with a hint of wistfulness but not a bit of reproach, was, "We should have impressed on you more how important it was not to leave the water heater on." They accepted my offer of some 1,800 shekels, $450 U.S., the most I could manage toward the repairs, and assured me that it was ample. I reeled from their candor and lack of vindictiveness. Though I beat myself up with guilt and remorse, from them I received nothing but the calm, friendly demeanor they had always shown me.

The following week, Ifat invited me to accompany her on her weekly round of nature workshops in local schools, in which she brought a new kind of animal to introduce the children to each time. As the children observed, held, and stroked the creatures, Ifat would tell them stories filled with information about noses or whiskers or sounds or habitats. That week, they were learning about rats, and

Ifat brought along a big mama rat and two baby rats. The children adored their gentleness, the softness of their fur, and the warmth of their plump little bodies. On our way home, we stopped in a nearby town to browse in the marketplace and to indulge in a *shawarma,* a local delicacy made of shredded lamb stuffed inside a hot pita and topped with a variety of salads and sauces. The whole day was a balm for me, helping to erase the horrors of the previous week's flooding and the pangs of guilt and remorse I still felt. By the time we started making our way back to the car, I had begun to feel that everything would be all right. It was a fleeting feeling.

When we got to the car, we found the mother rat dead and the baby rats dying in the backseat, victims of heat stroke from an hour and a half of baking in the unsheltered car under the hot midday Middle Eastern sun. We revived the babies by throwing water on them, then jumped in the car and raced for home. Halfway there, we ran over something sharp in the road and the tire blew out, nearly causing us to veer off the road. A passing motorist stopped and helped us change the tire, and we were on our way again . . . for a total of three minutes, until we ran over something else sharp, and the spare went the way of the first tire.

So, there we were: two ladies with two dying rats and one dead rat, hitchhiking on the side of a dirt road. As we waited for a lift, I struggled to remain calm and to quell the voices screaming inside my head, telling me that I was some kind of a curse, bringing death, doom, and destruction to anything or anyone who dared get close to me.

Pale beneath my Israeli tan and chilled despite the intense heat, I stood beside Ifat, imagining what she must think of me, afraid to look her in the face and see the judgment I was sure I'd find there, not wanting to see her regret over having ever met me, much less having extended such kindness to me, only to receive one disaster after another in return.

Finally I lifted my head and turned to her. She was gazing at me with the gentle face of friendship, her eyes lit with sincere affection. A slight smile played on her lips as she leaned her face close to mine and said softly, "It must be that we are meant to be very good friends." With those words, a great healing took place inside me.

Like Rami and Ifat's ceiling, which was long ago restored and upon which a second floor has since been built, our friendship has survived the rain and grown over the years. We did indeed become very good friends, and very good friends we remain.

—*Joy Pincus*

Tomato Soup
on Tuesdays

When I think of Mrs. Cochran, my mouth waters. January windows steaming from her saucepan on the stove, she'd heat milk while watching us from the inside out. She'd tap the glass at two flailing snow angels taking flight on her front-yard drifts. That was the signal that our hot cocoa was ready—or at least it would be, after we jumped in just one more icy pile, threw a few hard-packed snowballs, and stamped our buckled rubber boots on the kaleidoscope hook rug inside the back door.

"We're freezing to death," we'd shout, all red-faced and shiny, as we tossed our mittens, mufflers, hats, and voices up the kitchen steps to the lady wearing the cross-stitched apron.

"Honestly," she would say, her voice trying to match the seriousness of her face.

But we knew it was a bluff. We smelled the Nestle's and could almost taste the whirlpool of marshmallows freshly stirred in each brim-filled mug. So we'd kick off our galoshes, wrestle out of our damp leggings and coats, and race each other for a prize that two could win.

Mrs. Cochran loved us both. Cathy was her daughter. I was her neighbor, on the other side of the back fence. We'd both known her for the same amount of time, since we were born. Our mothers were friends, sort of—as friendly as two women can be when they've chosen completely different directions for their lives. My mom worked. Mrs. Cochran did not.

Instead, Mrs. Cochran canned peaches and shucked corn. She planted a garden with carrots and green beans. She made cakes for the church bake sale, cocoa with milk, and chocolate chip cookies you didn't slice from a tube. She was always home and always there. My mom had asked her to keep an eye on me. "Just until supper time," she'd told Mrs. Cochran, the September Cathy and I started first grade. So, every Monday through Friday afternoon, after the yellow bus passed by my street, I'd jump off at Cathy Cochran's stop and we'd go home together.

Without exception, two kisses were waiting at the door. Sometimes Cathy's was first; sometimes mine—pecks on the forehead as Mrs. Cochran slid our book bags from our arms.

"My, oh my! What do you have in there? A ton of bricks?" she'd ask, not seeing us lift our brows and our smiles, secret with the plan to one day surprise her with some bricks in our bags. We plotted it, on and off, for years.

We plotted lots of things, bouncing along on the green vinyl seats of Bus 15. We crouched low, pushing our knees against the metal backs of Jonathan Fisher and David Ramble, two neighborhood boys whom we outwardly hated but secretly liked, at least for a few years between eight and eleven. They'd toss spitballs over their shoulders, and we'd squeal, "Gross!" until the driver, Mr. Wiese, looked in his rearview mirror and growled at our giggling.

Cathy Cochran, the younger sister of boys off at college, was good in science and wanted more than anything to be a veterinarian. She liked to pet animals and owned a yellow bird, which refused to sing, a fact that frustrated, if not disappointed, Mrs. Cochran. We'd catch her rousing chorus of *Amazing Grace* or *How Great Thou Art*, performed at close and deafening range to the bird's cage. Of course, we'd laugh, almost pee our pants, and vow never, ever to be as silly as our mothers.

But then, my mother wasn't all that silly. In fact, she was serious and seriously glamorous, I thought. She wore flowered V-neck blouses, high heels, and hose that sometimes had runs she neglected to see. I liked her, though . . . thought she was pretty and important. I wanted to grow up and be just like her. It didn't really matter what I did, as long as I could wear lots of makeup, drive a fancy red car, and have somebody else worry about making dinner and ironing a stack of her husband's white cotton shirts just so.

Sometimes, I think of Mrs. Cochran in her apple green living room. I see her shaking water from an RC bottle onto the collar of dusty-blue denim, beads of slippery sweat kissing the line above her lips. The iron hisses its rebellion, and I see a faint smile, satisfaction, spread across her lips as she runs her hand smooth against the seam, then smooth against her brow. The box fan whirs warm air, and I, too, am satisfied.

Cathy and I would sit on the carpet for hours, playing the board game Life. Cathy's goal was to get more babies than she had in the last round; she ached to squeeze them in without restraint between the pink and blue pegs already snug in her plastic convertible. I always wanted to be the superstar, to live in the dream house, and to rack up extra points for building the better mousetrap. Cathy never went to college, always picked the card with the cheapest house, and refused, every single time, to buy insurance. She rarely won but never cared. She would insist that we play again tomorrow, her strategy and her skill unwavering.

I don't remember the last time that Cathy and I played anything together or even the last time we spoke. I outgrew the need for after-school care; I had my own house key. By ninth grade, our paths seldom crossed. She took vocational education and was in another building, her classes intersecting with part-time jobs that started at noon and left little time for socializing. I took college prep, made new friends, and learned more about the game of life. Sometimes I rode home in a Buick instead of a bus, getting off at my own stop. In the quiet of my empty home, I could eat whatever I found boxed in the cupboard, sneak sips of my father's Scotch and drags from my mother's discarded Dorals. I could put my feet on the couch and watch whatever I wanted on television, usually *Dark Shadows*, a show that Mrs. Cochran had never allowed.

"You'll have bad dreams with all that nonsense," she'd warn, flipping past the fangs of Barnabas Collins to find something more suitable, like *Let's Make a Deal*.

Along the way, over the years, she showed us how to crimp a crust and make play dough from Morton's salt. She punched out the itty-bitty purse and gloves for our Nancy Drew paper dolls and let us dress up in her church clothes. She sprayed Bactine on our scrapes and perfume behind our ears.

Mrs. Cochran was always the same—her smiles, her smells, the way she combed through our homework and brushed off our squabbles. Don't make mountains out of molehills. She refused to take sides. It was her Protestant predictability that both perturbed me and pleased me in that prepubescent way when love and hate ebb and flow side by side. Day to day, week after week, we knew the routine: tomato soup on Tuesdays and nickel-day Wednesdays at Kiddie Land when the Tilt-A-Whirl was the thrill of our summer.

Today, my husband is calling my name and asking if I am okay.

"Of course," I lie. I sit on the bathroom floor, gripping the toilet bowl, and wipe my mouth with a wad of wet tissue. I look at my swollen fingers; feel my swollen life. I am going to have a baby.

"Okay then," he says and kisses me through the door before rushing off to earn his living.

I call in sick; tell my boss it is the flu. I drag myself to the kitchen for more saltines and lukewarm ginger ale. I think of phoning my mother, but I don't. She had taken my good news between sips of coffee and hot breaths. I had tried to imagine her smiling, sitting in her Jacqueline Smith running suit, the uniform of the newly retired. "Oh, that's wonderful, honey," she'd said. "I'll watch her when you go back to work."

But I've got other plans. And they include lots of hugs and kisses, hot chocolate on chilly afternoons, and tomato soup on Tuesdays.

—Judi Christy

No Uncomfortable Silences

It has become a benign ritual sitting here at dusk, swatting mosquitoes and percolating yesterday's shadows through our thoughts. I imagine we do it to excavate our lost senses, to keep us vital in this passage of age we've entered. Wilfred's hat hides his drowsy eyes as he sways on the porch swing. He's tired, but he won't admit it. He's in the habit of playing Scrabble with Roy Kelly till late in the morning hours, always working to build his already abundant vocabulary. I tell him we're both in our seventies, and the words won't stick anyway. He sighs and drops his chin, peering at me through the reflection in his glasses.

"*Ambulate*," he says.

"I prefer to *walk*."

"*Interpolate*."

"I wish to *interpolate* the notion that you, with much affectation, are engaged in a foolish discourse you cannot win."

"That has *verisimilitude*."

"*Verily*."

The sun begins its drop behind the trees, and we sit in a silence that is shared by two people who have known each other all their lives. There are no uncomfortable silences, just a respect warranted by time, like two brothers aging across decades of life.

It was time for what Wilfred likes to call the "raconteur hour" of our evening, and I watch, waiting, knowing that like clockwork, he'll start up.

"Elliot, do you recall the whispering pines?" he says.

Of course I remembered.

"The Smoky Mountains, winter of thirty-four," he continues.

I stare at him, at those little gray eyes I've known most of my seventy-four years, like I've forgotten the entire thing. It irks him to no end.

"Tell me how old we were again, so I can do the math," I say.

"You were twelve. In dog years, seven years older than me."

We'd both been in Boy Scouts then, long before the war stole our innocence. We had a good troop here in the Carolinas. Our leaders, using the weekend camps as subterfuge from their domestic lives, showed us how to cook stew in tinfoil and how to carve sticks.

We were off on just such a weekend camping trip in the Smoky Mountains. It was winter, and a thick powdery snow hugged the ground. The trees wore white velvet; their branches looked like thin pins holding a foot of white snow against the blue sky. On the way up, our troop leader, a retired plumber named Lloyd Johnson, enlightened us about the whispering pines.

"And you believed it," says my friend. "The entire time." He laughs.

"And you didn't. Sure, you didn't," I say. "We all believed it, and not a one of us questioned it for fifteen years."

Then my memory plays back Lloyd Johnson talking about the psychology of the whispering pines.

> *Only in these mountains can you find the whispering pines. They're rare, very rare indeed. You see, these here pines are sensitive to human touch and emotions; they pick up on them. If you approach them very silently and take the needles of a branch in your hand and gently stroke them . . .*

With that, Lloyd held one of his big plumber hands palm-up and caressed it with his other hand like a baby, a smirk on his thin lips.

> *. . . well, that whispering pine will respond by swaying back and forth in the moonlight like it knows you. And if you listen real careful-like (here, he whispered deep in his throat) you can hear the whisper it makes as it sways.*

I recall shooting a surprised grin at Wilfred and him shaking his head at me like he didn't believe it. But he did, later.

"Not at first," says Wilfred, squinting into the setting sun, before turning his face to me and lifting his eyebrows. "I had my doubts. You know I analyze everything. Besides— Lloyd Johnson, the plumber? He was good at whittling sticks and cooking stew and fixing leaky faucets. But he was no horticulturist!"

No, Wilfred did not believe old Lloyd Johnson. Not right then.

Two nights later, we went to find the whispering pines. A heavy snow had fallen that evening, and Lloyd Johnson gathered all fifteen of us into the cabin living room. He was a heavy man with a thick turkey neck that shook when he spoke, burying his chin in folds of skin whenever his mouth opened. His tiny mouth was no match for his bulky form; in fact we often joked that God had stuck it on by mistake. He leaned on a cane he'd just finished whittling that, like all his other sticks, had a spiral handle that spun around into a ball at the top.

> *Boys, we are about to go searching for the whispering pines, a most mysterious tree here in the Smoky Mountains. We all will have flashlights, but once we get to the area, everyone must be silent and turn off all the lights, or we'll frighten them.*

Across the room, Wilfred raised a brow at me as he spun his flashlight in his hands.

> *The other scout leaders are already out there trying to locate the pines. Stay together!*

We walked through those silent woods on padded snow. The snow-laden trees formed a thick cottony fortress, their branches bent low to the ground. Our flashlights flickered over every object and into each others' faces. As the muffled sounds of our low whispered conversations hung in the frigid air, our breaths formed clouds of steam. We must have resembled a sloppy train trudging slowly through the forest, the steam-breath trailing behind us and twisting up to the bright night sky. When our voices got too loud, Lloyd Johnson was quick to turn his chubby face to us and quiet us by waving his gloved hands toward the ground.

Finally, after a thirty-minute hike, we stopped and huddled around the plumber. In front of us a gorge dipped into blackness, the other side lit by the moon, and the great pines cut a jagged horizon line. Lloyd hushed us, and when our chatter stopped the silence was powerful. You could hear clumps of snow falling from trees twenty miles away.

The plumber stood at the foot of an enormous pine, its needles coated with thick snow all the way to the top. The branches drooped heavily, the lower ones actually kissing the ground and forming a solid base.

Lloyd began in a whisper, steam rolling out of his mouth:

This is a whispering pine. We must keep quiet, because they are very sensitive to sound.

We looked at each other, and I recall those faces were set in frozen amazement, afraid to blink or move. Lloyd had us all. Including Wilfred.

Lloyd stood before us like Paul Bunyan, his fat Eskimo gloves gesturing, sweeping us in, and we the followers, the innocent students, the ensemble of idiots, watched as he lifted an arm and gently took a bough in his hand. With his other hand he stroked that branch and let fly with epithets of baby talk:

> *Nice tree . . . ah-huh . . . such a nice tree . . . yes you are . . . mmm-hmmm.*

And then, that tree moved. It swayed a little as if from the wind at first, and as he continued to coo and pet, it swayed back and forth like a great pendulum. Lloyd turned his proud face to his disciples.

> *See? He grinned. They are very sensitive to human touch. He turned back to the tree and gurgled some more.*

We took turns then, one after the other, under the careful guidance of Lloyd Johnson, stroking that tree's branches, talking to it like a baby cradled in our arms. It swayed so much that the snow fell from the top in a sprinkling of magical white dust onto our heads. Lloyd stood there with the other scout leaders, chortling like he knew something we did not.

After an hour of standing on that cold mountainside talking to a pine tree, we finally made the trip back to the camp. The group reverberated with an excited energy, as if we'd discovered an ancient secret that would forever change the course of boy scouting. The fifteen of us walked in leaps, chattering away about the way that tree swayed in the night sky as we stroked its needles. We stayed up late that night, whispering about making the cover of *Boy's Life*, as our flashlights bouncing off the cabin walls in a blackness filled with the bearlike snores of Lloyd the plumber and the other scout leaders. When we did finally sleep, we dreamt of wandering through the forest over a cottony white ground lit by the moon, surrounded by whispering pines that bent low as we passed, gentle giants watching over us in their world.

"Really had us, didn't they?" I say to Wilfred, as I watch him sip the last of his coffee. The setting sun lights the sky a bright crimson red.

"Until 1949, right before old Lloyd Johnson died," he says.

I look at him forgetful-like and say nothing, goading him to tell it again. Works every time. Here he goes.

"Yep. It was fifteen years later, guess I was twenty-five. I was back in Asheville for a family reunion, and there was Lloyd at the gathering, all hunched over on his cane. Time hadn't been at all kind to him. I sat next to him in the corner under a big pine tree. He looked at me and said, 'Wilfred Beems. You still pick your nose?' I asked him if he still carved sticks like a crazy fool. He held up his cane, and it had that curl handle that ended in a ball at the top. 'Last one I carved. Stroke,' he said. Then we sat there in silence, like there was nothing left to say. I glanced up at those pine branches.

"'Think it's a whispering pine?' I asked him. His face kind of turned to the branches, and then back at me; his mouth twisted into a crooked grin, and he let out a raspy, phlegm-filled laugh. Sounded like he was having a heart attack and couldn't breathe. Still laughing, he said, 'Could be, if you go get a thin yacht rope and tie it to the top, then go hide over there and get a group of Boy Scouts interested in talking to a tree.'

"I kind of froze then, just staring at his lined face, and for a moment I felt like a part of my childhood had been stolen. Then I said, 'Lloyd Johnson, you old son of a gun,' and laughed with him. We laughed so hard, everybody stared at us like we'd lost our minds. When I stood to go, he handed me his cane and said, 'I won't need this any-more.' He up and died two weeks later."

Wilfred looks over at me. I sit with my feet up on the railing and feign sleep. He shifts in his chair, annoyed, until I open my eyes and grin at him. And the silence con-tinues like that while the cicadas buzz in the trees, and then they, too, fall silent, respecting the space where nothing is said.

—*Timothy Agnew*

A Degree of Friendship

When I was a young woman, college was considered an option, not a necessity, for most girls. Many thought of going off to college as a desirable "growing up" experience and as a way to meet the "right" guy, the assumption being that you'd then marry him as soon as he popped the question. At least, that's the way my parents viewed my college education.

When I came home for the summer after my freshman year in college, still single and with no immediate prospects of a potential husband in sight, my mother said, "You know, we sent you away to school to find a nice man." And I had thought my folks wanted me to get an education—possibly to earn a degree. Even though my grades had been good, in my mom's eyes, I had failed—or maybe I was just on marital probation, with the passing grade, an engagement ring, expected the following school year.

During high school, I had talked about going to a small local college. Mother was firmly against that and insisted that it was time I "had the experience of living away from home." After her unexpected remark about my failure to land a mate during my first year away at college, I guessed what the real objection to the hometown college had been: She obviously thought that there weren't enough or maybe the right kind of men at that small institution.

In my junior year at the university, I did meet the man of my dreams—and promptly dropped out of school to marry. Looking back, I can't recall a single negative remark from either of my parents about my decision to leave school. But then, I'd done my job by finding that "nice man," sparing them the embarrassment of having an unmarried daughter.

My new husband and I stayed in the campus town, and I worked while he continued his studies. Some said I was earning my P.H.T. (Putting Hubby Through) diploma, but no one faulted me for it. In those days, it was considered more important for the man to finish school, and truthfully, I was content.

As the years passed, I found that people assumed I'd finished college. Even my kids thought I had a bachelor's degree. I never intentionally misled anyone into believing I was a graduate, but neither did I say I was a dropout. Though I sometimes felt wistful about my absence of a degree, I never regretted marrying early.

When my youngest child was ten and I was forty-six, a local university began holding credit classes at a shopping mall a few miles from our house. This unusual concept made the front page of our metropolitan newspaper. Caught up in the excitement of the story, I immediately called the school for more information. When no one answered, I realized it was only six o'clock in the morning—and I kept calling back until someone answered the phone.

At the shopping center classes, I met a number of people like myself: Women with college credits who had never finished their schooling because they'd married and had children. Shirley was among those women, and she and I took several classes together over a period of years. Then Shirley had an accident that left her temporarily unable to drive. It looked as though she would have to drop out of school. I offered her rides, she accepted, and soon we became out-of-class friends.

Eventually, I shared my big dark secret with Shirley.

Those first classes I took at the mall were purely for enrichment. I didn't think getting a degree was possible at my age. Then, after a while, I realized I was piling up so many credits that I probably could earn my bachelor's after all. The school approved my course proposal, and I was on track for graduation.

Still, I didn't announce my degree plans to anyone but Shirley. She, too, was struggling with studies and understood that something might come along to keep me from finishing the requirements.

My last semester arrived. Now graduation was finally something I could count on. Though I was bursting to tell my husband, I decided it would be even more fun to surprise him. On graduation day, I'd ask him to accompany me to the downtown ceremony. Perhaps I'd tell him I was going to see a friend graduate and wanted him to escort me. At the last minute, I would whip out my cap and gown—and enjoy seeing his shocked but happy expression.

Shirley and I talked about the graduation caper, and I knew she could keep the confidence. Then I got the bad news. That spring my son, Dave, who attended another university in the same city, also was graduating. I had looked forward to attending his commencement as much as I was anticipating my own. When I learned that his ceremony and mine were scheduled for the same day—and even the same hour—I was crushed.

Though I thought nothing could have kept me from attending my school's graduation program, there was no way I would miss Dave's big day. Shirley and I talked about the unfortunate conflict. She assured me I was doing the right thing. Sad as she would have been over missing her own graduation, she conceded that she, too, would have chosen one of her daughters' graduations over her own.

Dave's commencement day was a magical one. Our family had choice seats in the first row of the balcony, where we could get an overview of everything happening. During the recessional, I hung over the railing and caught his eye as he walked back up the aisle. My son gave me his biggest smile, and I was positive I'd made the right choice. There wasn't a moment of regret for me that Sunday.

The day after Dave's graduation, I came down from my motherly high. It had taken me thirty-two years to finish college, and fate had kept me from celebrating publicly. I had neither the diploma nor the keepsake program to symbolize my accomplishment. Even though I would be able to pick them up later, it just wasn't the same as having them handed to you. Also, now that the surprise element was gone, I had to figure out how to break my academic news to my family. It was not a good Monday.

Then the mailman came, delivering an envelope with Shirley's return address. Inside was a card she had customized to say, "Congratulations on Your Silent Graduation." I loved it.

Shirley had guessed how I'd be feeling. She knew I wanted a little recognition for completing my degree. I looked at the card a number of times that day, and then tucked it into my box of treasures.

—*Joanne Keaton*

Angel in Camouflage

The holidays had always been a difficult time for me. My father died on Thanksgiving, so while others celebrated with friends and family, I usually lolled in my feelings of loss. One year, I decided to do some volunteer work, not only to help those less fortunate, but also to try and distract myself from the inevitable sadness that accompanied the Yuletide spirit. I signed up to volunteer at a local children's hospital to help spread cheer to the kids who were not able to spend the holidays at home.

On my first day, I was full of jitters and fears. That afternoon I was to visit the bedridden children in their rooms and read to them. I had never really been around children before, let alone sick ones. I passed by the playroom, echoing with laughter, where volunteers were doing arts and crafts with youngsters and children were racing cars on the floor. I silently wished that I'd been given that fun task rather than reading to a child who was too sick to visit the playroom.

I was assigned to visit a little boy named Jonathan who was suffering from leukemia. As soon as my foot crossed the threshold into his room, I felt like an intruder and saw the reality behind the stark white hospital walls. Jonathan was staring at the television screen, where Fred Flintstone was up to no good with his pal Barney. At first, I sat quietly in the chair next to his bed. I knew he noticed I was there, but we were both too shy to speak. I also couldn't help staring at him, which I was sure made him uncomfortable. His small face was pale and sunken, and he wore a Dodgers hat on top of his hairless head. He looked much older than his eight years. I looked around the room for something to help me shatter this uncomfortable moment. Finally, I spotted a G.I. Joe doll on the nightstand and picked it up. Instead of his usual camouflage, Joe, too, was dressed in what looked like a hospital gown.

"What's wrong with G.I. Joe?" I asked. "Is he sick?"

Jonathan slowly turned his head toward me and said, "Yeah, like me." He then turned back to the television and continued watching the cartoon.

I was too choked up to read to him, so I just sat there in silence, watching television with him until our hour together was up. That night when I went home, I felt so empty inside. I kept thinking of the sick little boy in the Dodgers hat. He was so young, too young to be dealing with such hardship and an uncertain future. I wondered whether he understood what death was, and worried how anyone that age could possibly have the courage to face it. Jonathan both haunted and intrigued me, and for days I couldn't get his face out of my mind. Every time I thought of him, tears welled in my eyes.

During that holiday season of volunteering, I was

assigned to many different areas of the hospital. I held premature babies, sweet and delicate in my arms, and rocked them to sleep. I helped organize a group of little carolers who traveled through the hospital in wheelchairs and crutches, spreading holiday cheer to their fellow invalids. I even had several occasions to go into the playroom to make cardboard-and-glitter Santas and to build Lego villages on the floor. But each time I went to the hospital, I made a point to check in on Jonathan. I wasn't sure why he had such an effect on me—maybe because he seemed so accepting of his fate, while I was so afraid of mine. Ever since I'd lost my father, I'd feared death, particularly the death of others, more so than my own.

From my brief encounters with him, I could tell that Jonathan was a brave young man and that I could learn a lot from this youngster. It took a while for Jonathan to warm up to me. A quick hello and a handful of chocolates every time I went to see him finally did the trick. After a while, even though he never spoke to me, he would greet me with a smile and a blush, as if he was developing a crush on me.

One day I was assigned to read aloud to a group of children in one of the waiting areas. The children eagerly gathered round, and I opened the cover to begin reading about the little engine that could. Before the first word left my lips, I glanced up to see Jonathan in a wheelchair, eyes twinkling, anxiously waiting for me to read. It was the first time I'd ever seen him out of his room. After story hour was up, I wheeled Jonathan back to his bed, and for the first time since telling me that G.I. Joe was sick,

Jonathan spoke to me. He told me about his family, how his mother cried sometimes when she visited, and about his new baby brother who "isn't sick like me." He told me about how he used to love going to school with the other kids and how he missed playing in the park. Then he told me about his illness and that someday he was going to die. When he said this, I laid my head on the side of his bed. Jonathan softly patted my hair and said, "Please don't cry. When I'm an angel up in heaven, I'll come and visit you, just like you visit me."

That night when I got home, I watched *It's a Wonderful Life*. I'd seen the movie many times, but that was the first time I really understood it. For the first time, I realized that I should be happy with what I had and not saddened by what I didn't have. Aside from the yearly holiday blues, I loved my life and wouldn't have wanted it to turn out any other way. I missed my father and knew that nothing could replace his place in my heart. But I also recognized that my life might have been different, I might not have gone to college or met my husband, if my father had lived. Then I thought of Jonathan, and I wondered whether and how my friendship with him would change my life.

Christmas was an exciting day at the children's hospital. Santa and his elves came to visit, as did some local celebrities. It was so touching to see everyone light up with joy as Santa and the celebrities shook hands and sat with the children, asking how they were feeling and what they wanted for Christmas. Even the children who didn't celebrate the Christian holiday were included, shaking hands with the sports and television heroes, and feasting on holiday treats. It was an exciting day for all, and I wanted to share it with Jonathan.

When I got to his room, I found him sitting up in his bed, rubbing tears from his eyes.

"What's the matter, Jonathan?" I asked.

"Nothing," he said, but I knew better.

I sat on the edge of his bed and handed him a candy cane. He shook his head in refusal.

"Would you like for Santa to come by and see you?"

Again, he shook his head.

"This is Christmas; you shouldn't be unhappy," I said. "What will make you feel better?"

"My mom," he almost whispered.

I looked around the room, surprised to find that she wasn't there. Jonathan had been so excited about spending Christmas with his mom. He'd talked about it for days, but there he was, alone in his room, no mother, no baby brother, nobody but me.

"I'm sure she'll be here soon," I said, trying to comfort him. "It's still early." Glancing at my watch, I felt uneasy to see that it was almost four in the afternoon.

"She's not coming," Jonathan said, punching the mattress with his weak little fist. "My baby brother's sick, so she has to stay home with him. It's not fair! It's not fair! What about me? I'm sick, too."

"I'll stay here with you," I said.

Jonathan didn't answer, but I knew he wanted me to stay. So, I sat with him, watching television and talking about whether Santa was real, and I didn't leave until his spirits lifted and I finally saw him smile.

Because I had family visiting from out of town that next week, I didn't return to the hospital until after the New Year. On my first day back, I was assigned to the play-room, where I played checkers with a teenager who was recovering from a terrible auto accident. He won all three games. After my hour with the teen was up, I stopped by Jonathan's room to say hello, but he wasn't there. I figured he was probably with another volunteer, so I stopped by the nurses' station, where two nurses busied themselves with paperwork.

"Can you please tell me where I can find Jonathan Porter?" I asked a pretty redheaded nurse, who looked as though she had just come out of training.

The nurse glanced at me briefly, as though she was afraid to meet my eyes, and then turned to her associate for an answer.

"Are you a family member?" the older nurse asked.

"No, I'm a volunteer here," I said, stepping back from the desk so she could see my blue apron. "I've been vis-iting with Jonathan these past several weeks. I haven't been by his room since Christmas, and I just wanted to say hello."

"I'm sorry, but Jonathan passed away the day after Christmas."

I stood completely still for a few moments, hoping that the nurse would take back what she'd said. Maybe it was a mistake, maybe it wasn't Jonathan at all, but another sick boy who'd died. Maybe she was confusing him with another patient; after all, there were so many of them. But somehow I knew that it was true. Then I recalled our last visit and how sad he'd been that his mother hadn't come to see him.

"Was anyone there with him when he died?" I asked.

"Yes," she said, to my relief. "His mother came just a few hours before he passed away."

"Thank you," I said, turning away.

"Oh, miss," the nurse called out. I turned back. "Are you the volunteer he called his angel?"

"Yes . . . yes, I suppose I am."

"He wanted you to have this," she said, handing me the G.I. Joe doll I had spied on my first visit with Jonathan. Only now, G.I. Joe wasn't wearing a makeshift hospital gown; he was wearing his camouflage uniform. I hurried away from the nurses' station and went outside to the dark, quiet parking lot where nobody could see me. I looked up toward the heavens and lifting G.I. Joe into the cool winter air, I mouthed, "Thank you." And I knew my angel was watching, just like he had promised.

—*Theresa Marie Heim*

The Blarney Stone

I moved into my home in 1985 with three dogs, two
cats, and a truck filled with old furniture I had bought
at a store that billed itself as an antique shop but most
assuredly was not. I had invested every cent I had in the
down payment on the house, and I couldn't afford to buy
dinner much less hire a moving company. Instead, I asked
my young friend Kathleen to help me get settled. "Pack a
lunch," I'd said. "I'm facing some lean times."

Kathleen and I had met doing props for a play at a
community theater, and we bonded instantly. She was still
in high school, small, and very quiet. But she dwelled in a
magic world all her own, and her heart was filled with
music. Sometimes, when her inner melody became irre-
sistible, Kathleen would grab my hand and the two of us
would dance down Glendale Avenue as if a full orchestra
were playing on the lawn.

The morning of the big move, Kathleen appeared
loaded down with a sleeping bag, toothbrush, and a huge
green stone. The rock was so large that she had to make a
separate trip to haul it out of her mother's car. When she

arrived, I was attempting to leash the dogs and to cage the cats.

"I'm here," she whispered, tapping me on the shoulder. "And I brought you a wonderful thing."

My cocker spaniel was staring at the truck with a baleful eye. "You hold Jake's leash," I said. "Molly vomited dinner, and I need to give her a tranquilizer. She gets very gassy when she's tense."

"I brought you a *magical* thing," said Kathleen.

My baby kitten ran under the house, and I got down on my stomach to coax her out. "Can you grab Toby Ann?" I said. "She hates that cage. It will take both of us to get her locked in. Here, put on these gloves."

"It is *very* special, and it will make you happy," said Kathleen.

I finally heard what she was saying. "Kathleen," I said. "I won't be happy until Sunday morning when this project is over."

She tugged at my arm and pointed to the painted stone she'd dragged in front of the truck. "This will," she said. "Look."

"What is it?" I asked. "A grass substitute?"

Kathleen blushed. "Of course not. It's a blarney stone."

"But I'm not Irish," I said.

Kathleen laughed. "Tomorrow is St. Patrick's Day. *Everyone* is Irish on St. Patrick's Day."

"We can discuss that after midnight," I said. "Right now I have to get my little zoo organized and hit the road while the sun shines."

"The sun never shines in Pacifica," she said, picking up my poodle and dumping her in the front seat of the car.

"My real estate agent told me there is endless sunshine on the coast," I said.

"Real estate agents are like lawyers," said Kathleen.

"What does that mean?" I asked.

"You'll find out in about an hour," said Kathleen.

I looked at the stone more carefully then. It was immense, almost as heavy as Kathleen. It was painted with bright smiling figures dancing a jig and a border of shamrocks, flowers, and splashes of glitter. I took Kathleen's hand.

"This is a work of art!" I exclaimed. "Did you paint it yourself?"

Kathleen looked shyly down at her feet and nodded. "The fairies helped me," she whispered.

"Well, it's gorgeous, and I love it!" I said.

I tucked Cindy on my lap under the steering wheel and tried to adjust the rearview mirror. Kathleen held Molly, who was nursing a cold. Jake rested at our feet.

"I just hope she doesn't get sick again," I said.

We drove down the highway as quickly as I could manage. As soon as we got near the coast, fog enveloped us like a shroud. The road, the trees, the exit signs—all disappeared in a silver mist.

"See what I mean?" said Kathleen.

I leaned forward until my forehead nearly rested on the windshield, trying to peer into the blinding fog.

"This is just temporary," I said. "The weather forecast said sunny and clear."

"Watch it!" called out Kathleen. "You missed the Sky-line exit."

I backtracked, and when we got to the road my newly acquired house was on, I said, "Watch for four-four-one, Kathleen. It's on the right."

Kathleen's head bounced against the window, and she gripped the door rest to steady herself.

"I don't think you're driving on the street," she said. "It feels very bumpy."

"That's just the furniture tumbling around in the truck bed," I assured her. "I forgot to strap down the couch. Do you see a driveway?"

"I can't even see a house," she said.

That was when the first miracle happened. The fog lifted like a yoyo on its way up—and there stood my brand new home, illuminated like a magic castle.

Kathleen smiled. "Looks like the leprechauns got here before we did," she said.

"Sure they did," I said. "Let's unpack."

"First, let's put out the blarney stone," said Kathleen. "How about in the middle of the lawn?"

"I'd rather put it in the living room, so I can admire it," I said.

"Blarney stones are always outside," said Kathleen. "So the little people can dance around them."

"I see," I said. "Well, you put it where it will be the happiest, and I'll get started."

After depositing the elaborately painted boulder in "just the right spot" on my lawn, Kathleen played Irish jigs on the stereo to help us move faster as we unloaded the truck.

"You'll give the neighbors the wrong impression," I said. "You should have brought 'Hava Negila,' so they'd know what they are getting."

The hours flew by as the two of us sang and danced our way from chaos to order. It was the most fun I'd ever had, on a day I still remember as a highlight in my life. It was midnight when we put away the last dish and plugged in the last lamp, but my yard was still filled with moonlight.

"Look!" she said, pointing out the window.

I ran to the window, and I saw it, too. The lawn seemed to be teeming with hundreds of tiny green figures dancing around my blarney stone.

"Oh, Kathleen!" I breathed. "Are they . . . ?"

She nodded. "They've come to bless this house," she said. "You'll have the luck of the Irish for the rest of your days."

"Would they be offended if I put up my *mezzuzah?*" I asked. "Of course not," she said.

I took her hand. "Shall we?"

"Of course," she said.

And we danced the joyous step I've been dancing in this magic little house ever since.

—*Lynn Ruth Miller*

How Jack Got His Groove On

My younger son, Jack, went to a friend's birthday party recently. This might not have been so remarkable in and of itself, except that no one in our family knew that Jack had a friend.

"Jack's invited to a party?" My daughter Maria sounded incredulous. "Whose birthday is it?"

"Jacob, from my preschool," Jack said, more than a little proudly.

"Do you play with Jacob?" I asked. He nodded enthusiastically.

Now, before I go any further, I have to explain that Jack is a smart, loving, funny, and sweet child. What he hadn't been, up to that point, was social. Sure, he'd play with Maria and his older brother, Charlie, when they roped him in to whatever game they concocted, most of which required him to be the baby or the dog. But he was just as happy playing by himself.

My two older kids had altogether different social tendencies. Charlie had a string of friends who wove in and out of our house on a daily basis. For these older boys, our basement was the primo destination for computer games,

Nintendo, foosball competitions, and sleepovers. This same boys could be seen inline skating around the subdivision on warm summer days or shooting hoops on our driveway.

My middle child, Maria, had her own ever-expanding circle of friends. While with her at the mall and other public places, she'd routinely greet children I didn't know, introducing them as, say, Lindsay, who'd been on her soccer team two years ago, or Courtney, a cousin of a friend. She had two basic modes of action: playing with friends and making plans to play with friends. Her extreme need for socialization included actual physical symptoms of withdrawal when she couldn't have a friend over. I've known people trying to quit smoking who are less cranky.

Jack, unlike his older siblings, never talked about school. He never hounded us to go play with a neighbor kid or asked if he could invite another boy over to play. He never complained about being bored or wanting to go *do* something. At home, Jack seemed happiest putting a puzzle together or pretending with his action figures. In short, he was the perfect last child for a mother who was worn out from keeping up with the social lives of her two older offspring.

"Kids come to the door and want to play," I told my mother, "and he'll say, 'No thank you, I'm doing something.'"

"You were the exact same way at his age," she said. "Such an oddball. I never could figure you out."

Mom is such a reassuring presence in my life.

When the appointed day came, I drove Jack to the birthday party with a touch of trepidation. I was certain he'd want me to stay, although I had told him firmly that I wasn't going to. We pulled into Jacob's driveway in view of the front yard where the party was already in progress. "Jack!" two little boys yelled. Jack stood in the doorway of the van beaming like a returning hero, and then jumped down to join them.

I gave the gift to Jacob's mother and thanked her for inviting my son.

"Jacob really wanted him at the party. He says Jack's one of his best friends," she said.

Another woman joined our conversation. "You're Jack's mom? My son, Spencer, talks about Jack all the time. They're good buddies."

I wondered what other secrets my son had kept from me.

I was able to get Jack's attention long enough to wave good-bye. I watched him in the rearview mirror as I drove away. He held up remarkably well, jumping in a leaf pile with the other little boys in a brave attempt to distract himself from my absence.

When I returned two hours later, the party wasn't quite over.

"We still have a few things to do," Jacob's mom said apologetically. "If you don't mind waiting?"

Mind? It was the perfect opportunity to view my son in a social setting, to maybe get some ideas on how to help him come out of his shell.

"Guess what, Mom? We got to eat on the floor!" Jack said when he noticed me, confirming my suspicion that my son would have thrived during the Cro-Magnon period.

Then it was time for the birthday boy to open his gifts, and I held my breath, anxious to see how Jack would handle the intensity of the moment. The guests sat in a circle around Jacob, each one clamoring for him to open their gift next. As the excitement heightened, the circle moved closer to Jacob, who looked overwhelmed and oxygen deprived. Luckily, one of the adults practiced crowd control and restored Jacob's airspace. It was heartening to see that Jack fit right in, clamoring and crowing with the rest of the mob.

And when the cake was served, Jack ate just the frosting, just like all the other preschool partygoers. I was so proud.

By the time the group moved outside to smash a piñata to smithereens, I had begun to see Jack in a whole new light. I no longer thought of him as the friendless kid who was always on the edge of things. He was laughing and talking to the other kids as if he was one of them.

Jack was one of the first in line to swing at the piñata, a brightly colored star that apparently was made out of the same material as those black boxes on airplanes. Each kid swung at it four times with no discernable damage. Finally, Jacob's dad wrestled it to the ground and smashed off one of the star points. His wife shook out the candy, and the children swooped down like birds pecking at scattered breadcrumbs.

When it was time to go, I reminded my son to thank Jacob for inviting him. He did, and added all on his own, "See you tomorrow at school." Where did my baby get these social graces? I wondered as we walked to the van.

"Mom?" Jack said, interrupting my thoughts. "How come I never get to have a friend over like Maria and Charlie do? Can Jacob come to our house sometime and play? I want to invite Spencer over, too."

Clearly, Jack was getting the hang of this friendship thing.

I sighed. It was the end of an era.

—*Karen McQuestion*

Love Lessons

I tiptoed to the kitchen and placed my ear against the door. Inside, I heard a deep voice and then laughter.

My mother had a male visitor! Who was it? The only other male visitors to our home had been family—grandpas, uncles, and cousins. My curiosity finally got the best of me, and I peeked around the corner and stared in awe. Sitting at our kitchen table was a dapper gentleman wearing an Army uniform adorned with rows of medals pinned across the chest. His dark wavy hair was brushed back from his smooth forehead above two flashing brown eyes. It was his dazzling smile and beautiful white teeth that really sent me spinning. He was the most handsome man I'd ever seen. And the minute I saw him, a gap-toothed smile spread across my face.

My mother was a young widow then with three small children. My sister was ten, my brother four. I was six, and I missed having a daddy. Our father had been killed in a car accident. After a while, I realized he wasn't coming back from heaven, but in my childlike faith, I figured that since God had taken away my father, He could send me another one. So, I prayed and prayed for a new daddy, never doubting that God would hear my prayers and send one to me. Peering into the kitchen at the dashing soldier with the dancing eyes and brilliant smile, I knew he was the one.

"Thank you, Lord! Hallelujah!" I said, imitating Sister Riley. Then I marched right into that kitchen.

"Hi! I'm Patty. What's your name?"

"George," he said, flashing his pearly whites at me.

"Are you a hero?"

"No." There was that smile again.

"Then why do you have all those medals?"

"I've just come back from a war, and they gave me these for good conduct."

Looking toward Mom, who was making coffee, I asked, "Don't you think my mother is pretty?"

"Patty!" Mom scolded, her face turning crimson as she glanced at George. "Go outside and check on Benny."

George leaned forward and whispered to me, "Yes, I do. I'll see you later, Patty. I think we're going to be good friends."

George started calling on Mom more often. I don't think they went on many dates, and when he came to the house to see her, Mom had to share him with me. I would wait anxiously for my new friend to arrive and then rush to him with so many questions and things to say. He always seemed happy to see me and never grew tired or impatient with my endless questions. He played games with my brother, sister, and me, and when it came time for us to go to bed, I would refuse to go until George read me a story. Most of the time, he'd nod off in his chair after I'd pretended to be asleep.

In spite of me, Mom and George decided to get married.

I was so hurt when they didn't take me along on their honeymoon. I couldn't understand how George could leave such a good friend as me behind. But I was thrilled the day they returned, knowing my favorite friend would now be living with us.

After the wedding, we all moved to a farm. I loved animals, and it was a dream come true for me. For George, who'd never been married before, coming out of World War II and into a ready-made family took some adjusting. One evening was especially bad. Benny was throwing a temper tantrum on the kitchen floor. Annie was complaining loudly and clearly that it was not her place to take care of that spoiled brat. While showing off trying to help Mom, I had spilled a whole crock of buttermilk. Our dog, Freddie, in his hurry to lap up the milk, skidded across the floor and bumped into me, making me drop and break the crock, which had been in Mom's family for ages. George stood there with a dazed look on his face and muttered, "I must have been in shell shock to marry a woman with three kids."

Mom fled to their bedroom in tears, and George walked out the back door.

I hurried out to the porch. "I'm sorry. I'll be more careful next time. Please don't leave!"

He picked me up, and gently wiping my tears, he said, "We're the best of friends, right?" I nodded. "Well, friends never desert the people they love. Don't you worry, I'll always be here." Then he went in to console Mom.

It didn't take long before we three children started calling George "Pop." He approved of the name.

"You kids had a wonderful daddy, and I would never try to take his place. I'll make my own place."

And he did.

Pop made a point of taking us to visit with our dad's parents often. "I'm sure it eases their pain to see you children," he would tell us. Bringing comfort to my grandparents also made me feel better and needed. They, in turn, grew to love George as much as we did.

Pop didn't send us to church—he took us. I insisted on sitting by Pop and sharing a songbook. I loved to sing, even though I couldn't carry a tune, and I'd belt out the hymns at the top of my lungs. Pop said he didn't mind, but then, he couldn't carry a tune either. Sometimes, if the preacher was extra long-winded, I would fall asleep with my head on Pop's arm. Mom would scold that, just because I went to sleep didn't mean Pop could, too, to which he'd reply that he was just keeping his friend company.

Pop also taught us the meaning of work. He encouraged us to do a good job regardless of what the task was, and living on a farm, there were plenty of tasks to do. Pop never made us work—he worked with us, and made it a fun and educational experience.

Once I climbed up on top of the chicken house, thrilled at my daring and how far I could see. I ran across the roof, which made the chickens squawk. When I climbed down, there was Benny.

"I'm going to tell Pop! You're going to get in trouble!"

"You're a brat!" I yelled.

When Pop came home from town, Benny was waiting, and sure enough, he ratted on me.

"It's not nice to tattletale," Pop scolded Benny, much to my surprise. "Friends never tattle on each other."

"She's not my friend! She's my sister!" Benny yelled.

"Well, you're no friend of mine either!" I yelled back.

"If you can't be a friend with your brother or sister, how do you expect to be friends with anyone else? I want you two to treat each other as though you're best friends." He made us shake on it.

It wasn't easy to keep that promise. But to this day I count my sister and brother as two of my best friends.

On one trip to town with Mom and Pop, I asked for a pair of fancy boots. They had sold some livestock, and I knew they had some money.

"I'm sorry, Patty, but this money isn't mine to use as I please. Your mother and I have some debts to pay. When you owe someone money, the money in your pocket isn't yours. It belongs to the people you owe money to."

To this day, I make sure to pay all my debts before I spend money foolishly.

Pop always told us that friends don't tell each other's secrets or discuss one another's problems with other folks. We knew that we could tell Pop anything and that he would hold it in his confidence. We did, and he did. Pop was easy to talk with, and our talks always helped, because he was a patient, careful listener. I've tried to be a good listener in turn.

Pop was upset on my wedding day. He worried that my fiancé and I weren't good enough friends. "Love is good, but you need friendship in a marriage," he said. He was right. The marriage didn't last. When I married the second time, I was certain that my husband and I not only loved each other, but that we were also best friends.

Over the years, Pop has always been there for me, through many ups and downs. Whenever I've tried to thank him, he just smiles that marvelous smile and says, "That's what friends are for."

Pop is in his eighties now. I still go to him with my problems, including when we lost my beloved mother ten years ago. He's as good a listener and teacher as ever. His lessons in friendship are being passed along to my children. Recently, when he was honored at a veterans' hall of fame in our hometown, I found out that he was quite the war hero after all. He'd been through the invasion of Normandy, the Battle of the Bulge, and all over Europe.

Another gentleman at the awards ceremony asked if George was my father.

"Yes, sir," I said. "He is my Pop and my best friend."

—*Pat Curtis*

My Very Best Friend in the Whole Wide World

I recently spent a few days with my brother's family. Since I live several states away, I hadn't seen my niece and nephews for several months, and it was a joy to discover how they'd grown, what they were learning in school, and all about their friendships.

"Who's your best friend?" I asked my four-year-old niece, Emily, who had just started preschool. She wrinkled her brow in deep thought, then smiled.

"Rachel with short hair," she answered confidently. "And the other Rachel, the one with long hair. And Sarah. They're my best friends."

"But who's your one very best friend in the whole wide world?" I teased her.

She rolled her eyes at her seemingly slow-witted aunt. "They're all my best friends, silly!" she said, and jumped off my lap to play with her Barbie dolls.

That night, when I was putting Emily to bed, she asked me who my best friend was.

"Your mommy," I answered without hesitation.

"Why?" she questioned, and I smiled as I wondered how to answer such a big question.

Pam and I met when I was in eighth grade and she was in ninth. At first, I had a hard time understanding why this pretty, outgoing, popular blond girl wanted to pal around with a shy, skinny, unpopular brunette like me. Maybe it was our shared love of the Muppets, Rick Springfield, Swedish fish, and the Go-Gos. Maybe it was the way we could both spend an hour picking out fifty cents worth of candy at the penny candy store down the street or sing the jingles from a hundred different television commercials.

As the years passed, Pam and I remained inseparable, despite attending different high schools and living ten miles apart. We were as comfortable doing each other's makeup as we were having our infamous free-for-all food fights. We spent the summers together at the beach, and she spent every weekend at my house. We called each other every afternoon, and we shared clothes, secrets, and crushes.

When she was sixteen, she confessed that she was in love—with my brother, Greg. He finally noticed her, too, and they began dating. When she turned eighteen they got engaged, and they married straight out of high school. It seemed perfect: My best friend was my sister-in-law. But we'd already started drifting apart.

Pam was rooted in the farmlands and church community where my brother served as a minister. I was a single, free-spirited artist and college student, striving for the bohemian life of a Dorothy Parker or Anaïs Nin. Pam's letters to me were filled with her desire to have a baby, marriage, housework, and church potluck suppers; mine to her were filled with poetry, doomed love affairs, college classes, and tales of trying to write the great American novel in all-night diners. While she grew her hair out far past her shoulders and dressed in Laura Ashley prints and ballet flats, I cut my hair off to crew-cut length and stomped around in combat boots and ripped T-shirts. Though we no longer seemed to have anything in common, I still considered her to be my best friend. It was instinct, holding on to a piece of my past I didn't want to lose. More than that, I'd never found anyone to take her place in my heart.

Eventually my hair grew out, I became a freelance writer, and I fell in love with an architect. We were married in 1995. By then, Pam was a full-time, stay-at-home mom with two children and one on the way. Though our lives still couldn't have been more different, when it came time to choose my maid of honor, she was my first and only choice. She stood beside me like she always did, watching as I married the man I loved and laughing with me when her two-year-old son tore down the aisle during the cere-mony to ask his aunt to come play outside with him.

In the years since, our lives have sometimes inter-sected, but more often they've detoured away from each other. We now live eleven hours apart, and just when I left the corporate world to work at home, she started nursing school and working part-time outside her home. We still get together once or twice a year to grab a mug of tea and catch up. Within a minute or two, we usually pick up our conversation right where we last left it.

It is through these conversations that I've discovered it isn't our common interests that make our friendship so unique, it's our common history. It is seventeen years of laughter, tears, joy, and pain shared. Seeing one another at our best and worst has created an unconditional love and a bond that's grown deeper as we've moved from children to adults, from best friends to sisters.

Emily, I hope you find a friend who is as loyal, funny, smart, and kind as your mom—my very best friend in the whole wide world.

—*Victoria Austen Moon*

Brian's Gift

Living in a rural community usually doesn't afford young children the luxury of many friendships. My brother, Jim, and I were such children. Fortunately, we were close in age and enjoyed each other's company. But we relished any opportunity to ride our bicycles a mile down the gravel road to our nearest neighbors to play with someone our own age, a boy named Brian. His parents were farmers, and he had a large family of older siblings and one younger brother.

Having a friend close by made summers extra fun. One of my earliest and fondest memories of Brian is when we were about six and seven years old and played softball in the front yard, using a Frisbee for home plate. I can still see Brian, racing around the bases like a dust devil, barefoot.

Of course, our friendship wasn't restricted to summers. We all attended the same school and rode the same school bus. I don't remember the day or even the year when I first found out that Brian had muscular dystrophy, only that it was while we were still in elementary school. It seemed to happen suddenly. We were saddened to watch our healthy playmate grow increasingly weak and unable to do things he had enjoyed doing just the year before.

One first day of school during grammar school is etched forever in my mind. The school bus came to a stop in front of Brian's house, and we all watched in silent sadness as Brian struggled to get on the bus. Finally, a fiercely determined Brian literally climbed the steps of the bus on his hands and knees. On the last day of school the previous school year, he'd been able to board the bus with little effort.

As Brian grew older, his condition worsened, and he had to resort to using a wheelchair. He was never *confined* to a wheelchair, however. The chair became his legs, not his chains. He had retained his upper-body strength, so his parents purchased a three-wheeler that enabled him to get around the country back roads.

When Brian was about thirteen, he was driving his three-wheeler up the slight incline of our front yard when the machine suddenly flipped back, dumping him to the ground and landing on top of him. I ran to him, crying and screaming for help, wondering if he was alive. Hearing my screams, my brother came running, too. Brian's eyes were closed and he wasn't moving.

Sobbing, I patted his cheek and called his name: "Brian! Brian! Are you all right?"

Brian opened his eyes and with a smirk said, "Hey, set the three-wheeler up and put me back on!"

My brother broke out in laughter, and Brian joined him. He loved to make people laugh. He'd certainly pulled a fast one on me, and he enjoyed every minute of it. At the time, I failed to see the humor in his joke.

Eventually, Brian's arms also weakened, and it became clear that he needed another source of transportation. My mother came up with an idea, and my brother and I pitched in. We made up coffee cans labeled with his name and a request for donations. After distributing the cans around our little town of 1,500, we soon had enough money to buy Brian a golf cart. While other kids were getting their first car, Brian was motoring around in his golf cart, all the time, in all kinds of weather.

By the time we all reached junior high, getting Brian ready for and to school presented another challenge. He could no longer ride the school bus, and his growing height and weight made it very difficult for his parents to lift and move him. My brother was there to help. Every morning, Jim went down to Brian's house and helped him get up and dressed and into the van. Brian's mother drove them both to school, where Jim helped get Brian out of the van and into his wheelchair. After my brother got his driver's license, he took Brian to and from school in the van.

Jim never thought of Brian as a burden or as anything other than his friend. In turn, Brian was a steadfast friend to my brother. Year after year—winter, spring, summer, and fall—my brother diligently assisted Brian, expecting nothing in return but his friendship. They forged a bond of mutual affection and respect that would last a lifetime.

As the day of their high school graduation arrived, I discussed with Jim how this event might change Brian's life. I worried that Brian would now be alone. After all, Brian's primary socialization, aside from his family, had come from attending school. Jim assured me that he

would continue to see Brian often and that their friendship would last. My brother kept his promises. After high
school graduation, Jim took a job in the area and kept in
contact with Brian. Jim continued to help Brian when he
needed it, and, just as important, they continued to share
"guy time" together. In time, my brother married and had
three children, two boys and a girl. Brian never married
or had children of his own, but he was always a part of
Jim's family.

In his early thirties, Brian passed away. His memorial
service was held in a small country church packed with
family and friends. After the funeral, my brother and I
were asked to join an informal meal served to the family
in the church's annex. Reminiscing with Brian's family
brought back many wonderful childhood memories of a
boy who taught us how to accept challenges and to laugh
at the world.

Later that evening, I sat quietly at my parents' dining
room table, reflecting on Brian's funeral and his life. My
father pulled up a chair and asked how Brian's family was
doing. I told him about the day's events and the fond
memories we'd shared over the meal with his family.

"Jim helped Brian all the way through school and for
all these years afterward," I said to Dad. "He was such a
good friend to Brian."

My father looked at me strangely. "You missed the big
picture," he said. "Friendship is a two-way street. They
both gained from their friendship. It was Brian who taught
Jim what real friendship is and how to look past someone's
disabilities. He taught both Jim and you many lessons,

simply by being your friend. You are both lucky to have known him."

My dad was right.

Whenever I think of Brian, I never picture him in a wheelchair. I see him tooling over the fields on his three-wheeler, or puttering down a dusty road in his golf cart, or playing softball . . . barefoot.

—Cherri Melton Flinn

Love Sees No Color

I always knew that bad things sometimes happen to good people. I was aware that a person could be rolling along in a comfortable life one minute, and the next could be tossed into the dung heap, like Job in the Bible. I just never thought it would happen to me.

After the death of my husband, that is exactly where I landed—in a dung heap. My husband's illness had been debilitating and lengthy. As a trained nurse and his wife, I felt that no one else could give him the kind of care I could, and so did. In caring for him, I missed many hours of work and consequently lost my job. My health declined, and I was unable to return to gainful employment. Then I lost my home. Despairing and frightened, I moved from the beautiful home my husband and I had shared for many years into a small, somewhat rundown house in a seedy neighborhood. I bid farewell to my friends, my neighbors, and, most difficult of all, to the members of my church. Heartbroken and depressed, I viewed my situation as a dead end, rather than as a fork in the road.

I knew that, to preserve my sanity, I would have to

grab my bootstraps and pull myself up out of the gray funk that surrounded my every waking moment. The best way I knew to do that was to find a church. There were many churches in my new neighborhood, but few of my denomination. The one I finally found was a long way from my home and had only remote parking. I was having some difficulty walking, and the trek from the parking area to the church proved prohibitive. The pastor told me of another church closer to my home and suggested it might be more convenient for me. Because it was small and sat back from the road, I hadn't noticed it before. The pastor told me the denomination but nothing else about the church.

The first Sunday I attended service, I walked in the door, was greeted warmly by an usher, and was stunned to realize that I was the only Caucasian in the room. No one else seemed to notice. After the service, I was greeted by the pastor, a native Tanzanian, who invited me to share coffee, donuts, and fellowship with other members of the congregation in the hall. They embraced me with genuine caring, and that day, I experienced the Holy Spirit as I never had before.

Before long, I felt truly at home, and one day a member of the congregation suggested I join the choir. The church's choir was one of the most beautiful I had ever heard. The music was, to me, one of the greatest pleasures of attending the service. I have a strong, decent singing voice and had always sung in the church choir. I had been wanting to join the choir at my new church, but most of their songs were old Negro spirituals, uplifting gems gleaned from their past oppression, and I wasn't sure I'd be welcome. Once the invitation was extended, though, I decided to take the plunge and attended the rehearsal the following Saturday. It was one of the best decisions I have ever made. The choir welcomed me with open arms.

Shortly after I got my official choir robe, we were invited to perform at a church in New Orleans, a long drive from Tampa. The church would pay the motel and bus expenses, but each member would be responsible for meals. We were to park in a parking garage downtown, where Larry, the choir director, had obtained free parking for us, so we could all ride together on the same bus to New Orleans. I was still reeling from my financial reverses and found it impossible to come up with the money to go. I hesitated to share such a personal problem with anyone, but I pulled Larry aside and quietly told him of my plight. He said that no one should be left behind and assured me that he would personally see to it that I had the money to pay for my meals. I was relieved. I really wanted to go.

Nothing more was said, and the morning of our departure, Larry was so harried, I didn't want to bother him about his promise to cover my meals. For the time being, I had nothing to worry about, as our first meal was provided as a box lunch on the bus. The trip was wonderful. We sang, laughed, talked, and enjoyed one another's company. Hours later, we arrived at the motel, dusty, tired, and hungry. I was assigned to share a room with a nice young lady and her baby, who was an absolute delight.

After cleaning off the road dust, the group began to drift in twos, threes, and fours toward the nearby restaurant. I hung around outside the motel room door, praying I didn't look as pathetic and misplaced as I felt, and hoping that Larry might walk by and, seeing me, remember that I had no money. He never did. Though starving, I was about to give up and go back into the motel room. Just then, one of the choir members, an older man with a built-up shoe, a cane, a pronounced limp, and a beautiful smile, walked up to me.

"Hi," James said, reaching out his hand.

"Hi," I said as I shook his hand. The conversation halted; I didn't know what to say. I was so afraid he would ask me to join him and his sister, Ella, for dinner. I couldn't even pay for a cup of coffee.

"I would be honored if you would let me buy you dinner."

I was stunned. This handicapped man who lived on a small fixed income and shared a home with his sister and her grandchildren so they all could afford a roof over their heads was reaching out in my time of need. I didn't even know whether he knew I was in need, but I graciously accepted his invitation, and I had a wonderful time. It was one of the most memorable meals of my life, not only because of James's generosity in treating me to dinner, but also because his and Ella's companionship fed my soul.

The concert was great! We sang our hearts out and received a standing ovation and several requests for encores. In appreciation, the church where we performed gave us a genuine New Orleans–style buffet in the school cafeteria before we boarded the bus for home. Thank God, I thought. No more meals to worry about.

On the bus ride home, Larry gave us a piece of bad

news: The parking wouldn't be free, after all. It would cost twenty dollars for each car. A large knot of panic rose in my throat. I didn't know what I was going to do. The closer we got to the parking garage, the more despondent and panicked I became. Still, I said nothing to Larry or anyone else. My pride just wouldn't allow me to fess up and ask for help. I preferred to suffer in silence and to send up some frantic prayers. My thoughts were interrupted by a tap on my shoulder and a gentle voice.

"Could you possibly give me a ride home?" James asked me. "Ella has to make a stop on the way, and I am so tired. If you would, I would be happy to pay for the parking. It would cost me more than that to take a cab."

Once again, I'd been saved by an angel—one with a built-up shoe, a cane, a pronounced limp, a winning smile, and a heart so big I don't know how he manages to carry it inside his small body.

In time, I found out the nature of James's disability. He had grown up in a poor area of Alabama at a time when segregation was a way of life. As a youngster, he had fallen from a tree and fractured his hip. The hospital had refused him service because he was black, a heinous policy made all the more heinous by the fact that the hospital had the legal right to do so with no repercussions. The fracture had healed in its own fashion, and the kind young man grew up unable to walk for many years. Eventually, a hip replacement put him back on his feet, but because one leg is several inches shorter than the other, James walks with great difficulty and lives in constant pain. Yet, he harbors no bitterness or resentment or desire for revenge. Despite the bigotry that cost him any possibility of a normal life, my friend is totally devoid of prejudice and hatred.

Several years after our choir trip, I asked James how he'd known I was flat broke that day in New Orleans. He just smiled and said, "I didn't." I've never believed him.

Over the years, James and Ella, a lady with the same beautiful, giving heart as her brother's, have bailed me out of many tough spots while I got my life back on track. They have always been there to steer me in the right direction when I've teetered off the path, and to lend their shoulders to lean on and their arms to protect me when it felt like everything was about to cave in. They've cared for me when I've been at my lowest, asking absolutely nothing in return. Because of their friendship, I have reentered the world as a valuable human being with hopes and dreams again. Through them, I have learned to accept my fate, not as an act of a vengeful God, but as a part of living.

James wasn't trying to buy my friendship that day. He didn't need to. He is greatly loved by anyone lucky enough to know him. I feel very fortunate to have known both James and Ella and, more important, for the privilege of calling them my friends.

—*Judith E. Dixon*

Sitting One Out

We met in a support group for parents of children with special needs. It was introduction night, and stories of heartbreak enveloped the room as one parent after another discussed their child's diagnosis and uncertain future, and the difficulties that both the children and the parents faced.

I spoke of my developmentally disabled fifteen-month-old daughter, Meredith, who could not yet speak and could barely crawl, let alone walk. Deciding that helping my daughter learn to walk and talk took precedence over my career aspirations, I had stepped off the ladder leading to management and left my position at a newspaper. I was feeling lonely and displaced. My old friends didn't know what to say, so they said nothing, and then they moved on. I'd leave my daughter's playgroup in tears after watching her silent struggle to move an inch, while her peers breezed by her, running to and chattering about their next discovery.

As I poured out my heart to the support group, there were sympathetic nods. Two other people made their introductions, and then it was Tonie's turn. She had twins, she said: Her daughter, Madison, had delayed speech, and her son, Griffin, had autism. She described a little boy who had to be watched constantly. He would scale the family's entertainment center and eat the wood shelves along the way. He had a penchant for running away at lightning speed, usually with no clothes on. One time he was found naked in a neighbor's pickup truck. Tonie was the main breadwinner in her family. Her singer/songwriter/carpenter husband spent most of his time working on his music, and with only her state agency job as their primary source of support, they often lived paycheck to paycheck. Yet, as she told her story to the group, she infused it with humor, and it was clear that somehow she found joy amidst the sorrow, and hope amidst the challenges. I knew I'd found a friend.

Tonie and I began to socialize outside the group, sharing our trials and triumphs, however small, and always sharing laughter as well as tears. At the end of the summer, after the support group ended, we continued to talk on the phone and to see one another. One night over margaritas, we spent three hours getting to know one another, each taking twenty-minute turns telling each other about ourselves. First I'd go, then Tonie. By the end of our talk marathon, we were marveling at the odds of us having met and become friends.

I was a sorority girl with a trust fund, who had been a Texas debutante. Of course, I explained, no debutantes anywhere else in the country bowed quite like us—"Honey, we did the Texas dip, a full bow with our heads touching the floor." It took grace, strength, and a sober escort to carry that off. I had married an attorney, and we lived in the hills with a Honda Accord and a Ford Explorer in the garage.

Tonie shared stories of her Cuban roots, of being a first-generation American, and of having been the lead in local plays. When she met Billy, her husband, she'd been engaged to another man. Smitten, she'd broken off the engagement and moved to Madison with Billy. A short time later, they moved back to Austin, and Tonie was pregnant with the twins.

My new friend was passionate about poetry and theater; I kept a private journal about my struggles with Meredith. Tonie greeted friends with a kiss; I stiffly held out a hand. We lived on opposite sides of town in vastly different lifestyles. But we both liked chocolate, and we both loved our children. For whatever reason, the universe had brought us together—and soon the circle of friendship included our husbands.

Just months after meeting, we got our guitar-playing husbands together, and before long, my husband, Jim, joined Billy on stage. Normally I was content to just groove in my chair at gigs; Tonie taught me to abandon my debutante skin and dance—with her! And she loved to flirt. I was in my mid-thirties and had long since forgotten what it was like for a stranger to offer to buy me a drink, but not Tonie. I loved watching her dance with lonely cowboys and use her mesmerizing deep-brown eyes to cajole free drinks from bartenders. I was still working on shedding my career-girl image, and Tonie in her retro, thrift-store ensembles was my glitter-dusted alter ego.

We'd dance and talk and laugh, and for a while, forget about our troubled lives . . . almost.

Like a persistent picnic fly, our worries over our children were always there, sometimes just below the surface, but more often, full in-our-face center stage. Many days we cried together. Some days, we'd celebrate—like when Madison started carrying on conversations and was no longer considered speech delayed. Then there was the day when Tonie's son, Griffin, and my daughter, Meredith, interacted. We don't know what the two were communicating that day on the floor in their silent world, with their heads together and making full eye contact with one another. We only know that it made them both smile. It was a day that glimmered with hope among so many days of uncertain darkness.

When the support group started up again in the summer, we both decided to go back. The group was held at a school for children with disabilities, some of them life threatening. Before the meetings, Tonie and I would sit in a tiny, beautiful memorial garden in the back of the school and talk. While other friends might meet over coffee, we met on benches dedicated to children who never saw their third birthday. It was a strange world we were living in.

Several years have passed since Tonie and I first met. I've had another baby, and Tonie is getting a divorce, so our dancing at gigs has waned. Though we don't see each other as often as we used to, Tonie remains my guiding spirit. Across town, she continues to work at her social agency job and to care for a troubled little boy who is beginning to find words. I remain at home, researching and trying every therapy possible to help my four-year-old to walk and talk. Tonie and I exchange e-mails, phone calls, and occasional Sunday visits. Tonie is still the mom I most want to be around, and her sense of humor still lights my life. But she doesn't laugh when I read entries to her from my journal. She still writes poetry, though.

The other night I went to see her compete at one of her "poetry slams," which aren't so much people reciting poetry as they are people sharing intensely personal experiences. Sometimes the performances are funny, sometimes cathartic. In the bright stage lights, I couldn't see Tonie's face well, but the outline of her red blouse illuminated the stage as she cleared her throat and began her poem, titled "Unspeakable." She shared the story of the silent inner world in which her son, Griffin, lives. While others were getting a poetic introduction to autism, I was running a movie reel through my head of all Tonie and I had been through with our children. In another poem, she spoke of the end of her marriage, and I felt as if a whole room full of strangers was listening in on our private conversations all those afternoons at Tonie's house. She spoke of the songs on her ex-husband's new CD that had been written about her. The rims of my eyelids could barely hold in the tears.

After her performance, she walked back to our table, leaned toward me, and said, "Am I killing you yet?" Laughing, we headed to the bar where we'd spent many nights dancing to those songs her husband had written. This time, we weren't going to dance. We were simply two mothers, two friends, taking comfort in sitting one out, together.

—*Sarah M. Barnes*

Somebody

In May 1993, just before I turned nineteen, I scored a summer job waiting tables in midtown Manhattan. I had returned to Long Island for the summer, intending to work double shifts through mid-June, long enough to accumulate the funds I needed to spend the rest of the summer on the road—more specifically, on whatever road led to the next Grateful Dead show. The restaurant where I worked catered to the business crowd, and 2:00 to 5:00 was break time for the waitstaff. During those three hours between shifts, I explored the city I had known my whole life but had never experienced as an adult with a little money in her pocket.

Within a few days of starting the job, I saw an opportunity to do some good. Each day I worked, I was granted a shift meal, but I rarely wanted to eat the same food I served day in and day out, and I could afford and preferred to buy a sandwich in Bryant Park. Since my restaurant was right down the block from Penn Station, where a homeless man had come to my rescue the previous summer, I figured that even though my shift meal didn't appeal to me, it would be a king's feast for someone on the streets. So one day, after the lunch crowd had petered out, I went into the kitchen and packed myself the heartiest meal I could fit into a take-out container, and off I went.

I arrived at Penn Station with my package full of food and plastic silverware. Half an hour later, after being snubbed by the very people who were used to being snubbed by passersby, I still sat with the package in my hands, no doubt pouting at the resistance I had met. I didn't realize anyone had noticed me until a tiny hand touched my shoulder and a pair of ratty sneakers came into my view. I looked up as a woman, about ten years my senior, with lips like chipping plaster, squatted beside me.

"Here," she said, reaching for the bag with dirt-caked fingers. "I'm not hungry, but they'll take the food from me."

Still disheartened, but unwilling to waste food, I handed her the bag. I watched as the mousy woman, who stood about five feet, if that, handed the meal to the very same man who had turned up his nose at me moments before. She smiled and waved at me as if she was beckoning to some long-lost childhood friend. Had she looked back, she might have seen the smile I returned, but she disappeared around the corner before I had the chance to even say thanks. The gratitude I felt at that moment seemed strange and quickly transformed to guilt. It seemed wrong somehow that someone in her obviously destitute situation was compelled to comfort me.

A few hours later, I unexpectedly got my chance to thank her. The trains to Long Island run an hour apart during off-peak times. After work that night, I missed my

train by seconds and spent the remaining fifty-nine minutes until the next one came smoking cigarettes and
writing in my journal on the steps of Madison Square
Garden. As I emerged from the station onto Seventh
Avenue, my eyes were immediately drawn to the woman.
I recognized the torn jeans, which looked five sizes too big,
and the thick gray sweatshirt, which made me perspire
just looking at it. She sat against a wall, her knees pulled
tightly to her chest and a cigarette dangling from her lips.
At first when I approached her, she extended a tattered
coffee cup that jingled with a few coins. When I got close
enough for her to recognize me, she straightened her spine
and rested the cup at her side.

Though time and my own powers of interpretation
have convoluted many of my experiences and conversations, I can remember our first exchange as if it had happened moments ago. Her name was Debbie, and her
handshake was much firmer than I imagined it to be. She
asked about me, and I told her I was an art student and
was waitressing to save money for travel. When I specu-
lated about the possibility of quitting school to become a
full-time Deadhead, a sort of motherly conviction
replaced her gravelly, noncommittal tone.

"Don't you dare give up on school," she warned, wag-
ging a skinny finger at me. "And stay off drugs."

I laughed, not at her seriousness, per se, but more so at
her sudden transformation. What she said next really
struck me. The look on her face went from one of warning
to one of grave knowing—the kind of look you'd expect
from a grandparent who had survived the holocaust. This

look alone prompted me to listen as closely as if she were Jerry Garcia himself. She spoke quickly and determinedly, like when you eat something that tastes awful, but you know is good for you.

"I didn't stay away from drugs, and they ruined my life. I lost my children and my family, and now I'm here, dying of AIDS." Though saying the words seemed to offer Debbie some relief, they hit me like an eighteen-wheeler doing ninety. We sat without talking, smoking my cigarettes, for what seemed like a week, Debbie's confession resounding in my head so loudly that New York City fell silent. I bought her a cup of coffee and got on my train.

For the next month or so, Debbie and I shared sandwiches, stories, ideas, dreams, and laughter. We also shared some tears, but I usually saved mine for my train rides home; I didn't want her to think I was spending time with her out of pity. I truly enjoyed her company and thoroughly valued the lessons she was eager to teach. I did what I could to make her life more comfortable: a pair of shoes, a new toothbrush, lots of coffee. I even helped her "campaign" for "financial assistance" from the yuppies who passed through Penn Station with such regularity that they were numb to the sight of struggling human beings. I had been forced to panhandle only once in my life, when I ran out of gas and my credit card was maxed out. It was one of the most shameful experiences I'd ever had, and seeing what Debbie went through to avoid "the system" baffles me to this day. But I never asked why she didn't take advantage of resources that were available to her. My role was that of a friend, not a social worker.

Finally, the time came for me to spread my wings and take to the road. Debbie didn't seem overly sad that I was going, I think mostly because she'd become accustomed to loss in her twenty-something years on this planet. My excitement over the adventures before me lessened my own sense of loss. We agreed that we were lucky, even blessed, to have stumbled onto such an unlikely friendship, and we promised to keep each other in our hearts. I gave Debbie a phone number and address where she could get in touch with me. Not surprisingly, she never wrote or called.

Several months later, just after the start of my sophomore year of college, I took a trip home for a long weekend to see Jerry and the boys play at Madison Square Garden. One night, in the midst of the chaos that always marks the end of a sold-out Grateful Dead concert, my friends and I were rushing through the crowd to catch a train. As we made our way through the masses of dread-locked heads and tie-dyed shirts, I heard someone call my name. Since about one in every ten girls born between 1970 and 1980 are named Jen, I chalked it off as a cry for some other gen-exer. But when I looked around to make sure, I spotted the only person sitting on the ground.

When I told my friends to hold up, they rolled their eyes and pointed to their watches. I started to swim against the current, trying to reach my friend, who was extending her arms toward me. At that moment, I felt like I was in one of those cliché dreams, walking down a long hallway, trying to reach a door at the end that keeps getting farther away. My destination wasn't a door; it was a familiar face that was warped with profound illness. The whites of Debbie's eyes were filled with blood, and welts covered her frail, out-stretched arms. When I got almost close enough to touch her hand, my friends shouted my name. I turned to signal them to hold on one more minute, but I could no longer see them in the crowd, which overwhelmed me with panic. I quickly mouthed the words "I love you" to Debbie, and she mouthed back, "I love you, too." I turned and ran, as much to find my friends as to escape the pain and horror of seeing Debbie like that. I have never quite forgiven myself for that decision.

The next summer, I returned to my job at the restaurant, and on the shift break my first day back, I packed up some food and headed down Seventh Avenue for Penn Station. I saw some familiar faces, who this time accepted the food I brought with gracious thanks. One special face was missing. I guessed the smile I had come to love no longer blessed this earth. Then again, maybe Debbie had finally sought help and was resting comfortably in a bed somewhere. The part of me that believes that scenario is the one that will one day put a dollar under my daughter's pillow on the night she loses her first tooth. It is the part of me that became a better person when I looked into the eyes of a nobody and saw somebody.

—*Jen Sotham*

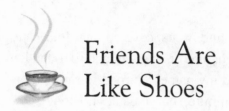

Friends Are
Like Shoes

s my fortieth birthday approaches, inevitable as a new hairdo, I realize how many women friends I've had over the years. Most have come and gone with the fluctuations of life, just like the latest shoe fashions waltz in and out of my closet.

Some of my friends, like some of my shoes, were silly mistakes that ended up in the Goodwill—or rather, good riddance—pile. They never did fit properly, and they always felt slightly "off," no matter how hard I tried to fit my tootsies into the glass slippers. Others were my absolute favorites for a while, but they wore out or wore off. All style and no substance; the quality just wasn't there.

Then there are my true friends—the ones who, like a pair of fine shoes, never go out of style or out of favor, whose appeal and value just increase with wear and time. These are the friends who stay in touch and stand by me—as if they and I have never gone off to a new state, a new job, a new husband, or, scariest of all, to become someone's mother. Physical distance does not separate us; time does not change the fundamental fact of our friendship; the wear and tear of life does not stop us. The sole still supports us; the colors and lines still please us; the uppers, still strong but grown supple, gently bend around our contours and ridges. Our connection is securely fastened, unaffected by the whirlwind of changes we've each been through, even when life carries us in different directions.

It may seem odd, this comparison of friends to shoes— but as any fashion-conscious woman knows, the right shoe, like the right friend, finishes the look, makes us whole. Though I hesitate to reduce my best friends to the level of leather and laces, if the analogy fits . . .

Deborah is the quintessential *peau de soie* evening shoe, regal and lovely. She appreciates the finer things, chooses only the best, and still looks polished long after the rest of us have drooped. She is a study in understated elegance and knows the difference between bone, beige, and winter white. From this sublime treasure, I've come to recognize my own appreciation for the finer things in life—and to the realization that I deserve them.

Janet is that pair of essential, timeless pumps that I wear often and would be lost without. Her sensibility is reassuring, her infatuation with discovery contagious. With this smart and spry classic, my basic needs and comfort level are assured—leaving me time and energy for fun. I can move gracefully from day to night, from work to play, from jokes to thoughtful discussion. My step is light, laughter comes easily, and I'm ready for adventure.

DeDe, my youngest friend, is funky, fun, and cutting-edge fashionable. She's that pair of "in" sandals I adore but don't need. They cost more than I think I can afford, but I can't resist—and they end up being worth every cent, surprisingly perfect for all occasions. Every time I wear them, I have a blast and try something new. More than just a good time, these jazzy little gems are fundamental to my happiness.

Sue is pure light and vibrant color. Her off-the-wall humor attracts attention the way a pair of lime green suede Hush Puppies does. Behind the zaniness is a sure-footer I can rely on and laugh with, out loud and often. These outrageous puppies sometimes surprise me, but they've lasted more years than I can count and still look great and feel good. They remind me to lighten up when I'm taking myself too seriously. On days when nothing seems amusing, they bring a slow, comforting smile to my face.

Georgiann is my pair of standard white Keds—familiar, comfy, and good for all seasons. I've had them since for-ever. They are part of my childhood. They take me home, and I'm a kid again diving into the ocean on a hot summer day. They have been up fool's hill and through the muck with me. They keep me moving forward, even when put-ting one foot in front of the other feels like the hardest thing I've ever done. I know I can slip into them tomorrow and all the days after. I am indebted to these lovingly worn sneakers.

Wendy is my one-of-a-kind, irreplaceable, European designer heels—distinctive and sophisticated, yet totally lacking in pretense. At first, I didn't think I could pull it off, such *savoir faire*, but this delightful indulgence suits me just fine. With these beauties, I stand up straight. I move more slowly, deliberately, gracefully. I speak with greater forethought and care. I am witty and completely present. Life is glorious.

In the shoe rack of life, these are the friends I cherish. They are the base upon which I stand, and they accompany me on my chosen path, regardless of where it leads or how bumpy or winding it gets. They are an exact fit, my perfect complement, and always within reach when I need them or simply want the pleasure of their company. These friends fill my life like shoes fill starlets' closet—and I am all the richer for them.

—*Donna Marganella*

A Midwest Miracle

Quentin Merkel is not a man easily moved to tears, but twenty years ago, he found himself crying late at night.

Two years earlier, his wife, Sharon, had been diagnosed with a debilitating disease that was robbing her of the ability to do even the simplest household tasks. Her prognosis was grim. She had amyotrophic lateral sclerosis, ALS, a degenerative, fatal disease that wastes away the muscles.

Exhaustion had set in for Quentin. He was working full-time as a high school teacher and coach, then coming home to cook, clean, and care for the Merkels' five young children and his increasingly ill wife. His day would start before dawn, getting every kid up and dressed and out the door before 7:00 A.M. It would end at midnight, after a full day's work, followed by dinner, dishes, homework, baths, laundry, and caring for his beloved Sharon. Every night, he'd fall into bed and cry and pray. He prayed for strength to keep going, fearing that he could not. He prayed for help, night after night, but none came, and he began to wonder whether his prayers would ever be heard.

One morning at school, fellow teacher and friend Leo Schultheis approached Merkel and asked, "How is your wife? Do you need help?"

"No," said Quentin. "We're fine."

Later that night at home, a deeply fatigued Quentin began his prayer again. That's when he got his answer. It went something like this: "Who the heck do you think you were talking to this morning? Here you are, asking for help from above, and help is being offered by someone standing right next to you."

When Quentin returned to school the next day, he told Leo the truth: Things were bad and getting worse. In response, Schultheis and his wife, Marilyn, began Project Merkel, the genesis of an amazing effort that continues today. It began as a group of volunteer adults and teenagers who cooked dinner, did laundry, bathed children, and helped with homework and housework. The sicker Sharon Merkel got, the more tasks they took over.

That Sharon Merkel is still alive and at home today surprises people who are aware of the cruel reality of her disease. Many know it by another name, Lou Gehrig's disease, coined for the 1930s-era New York Yankees baseball player who died from it at age thirty-eight. With ALS, the nerve cells that control the body's motor functions degenerate, and paralysis eventually sets in. Many of its victims die from pneumonia, unable to cough off congestion in the lungs.

Sharon was diagnosed with the disease in 1981, when her youngest child was a year old. It began with muscle weakness. Within a few years, she was in a wheelchair. Twice over the next four years, she fought off what she and her family feared would be fatal pneumonia. After the second bout, which put her in the hospital for four months, her family had an excruciating decision to make. Medical advisers were pushing them to put Sharon in a nursing home. They told Quentin that he wouldn't be able to take care of his wife at home, that if he put her in a nursing home, he could get on with his life. Quentin recoiled from their suggestion. Sharon *was* his life! He'd vowed to love, cherish, and take care of her in sickness and in health, till death parted them, and he wasn't about to back out on that sacred promise.

It was not an easy promise to keep. Raising five children on a teacher's salary was a stretch to begin with. Sharon required around-the-clock care, and the equipment she needed was costly, beyond what insurance would cover. Requests for help from the government were turned down; Quentin made too much money for his wife to qualify for Medicaid or other government assistance. She couldn't get help from the Social Security Administration, either. The purpose of the benefits, they were told, was to replace the earnings lost when a worker becomes disabled. The irony was appalling. Sharon hadn't been "working" before the disease struck; she'd only been raising five children.

Once again, friends stepped in. They assured Quentin that they'd find the money to keep Sharon at home. A small group of people set up a fund, dubbed it the Friends of Quentin and Sharon Merkel Committee, and began asking for contributions. Every year since, they've raised the money needed to pay for her care. The cost now exceeds $70,000 a year.

Sharon is now almost completely paralyzed. She is

totally bedfast and dependent twenty-four hours a day on a ventilator and other medical equipment, which require continual monitoring. Three trained caretakers take turns by her side night and day.

But her mind is sharp and fully engaged. She communicates by blinking out messages using an alphabet chart that two of her sons rigged up for her. Family and friends say she is still the heart of her household, still directing the daily traffic of family life from a bed in the living room, still the mom of the house. Not long ago, her youngest son, Shawn, came home later than expected, only to find his mother waiting up for him; she gave him a royal chewing out. Against the medical odds, she's survived to see all five children graduate from high school, two of them graduate from college, and one get married. Her life, though difficult, has been fuller and longer than the experts and strangers would ever have thought possible. Of course, they don't know Sharon Merkel's tenacious spirit and friends.

For more than two decades, scores of people have contributed staggering amounts of time and money to keep Sharon Merkel alive and in her home, and to keep her family afloat and together. Over the years, people have often asked Quentin Merkel whether his family has ever prayed for a miracle. A soft glow seems to light his face as he answers quietly, "We did, and we got it. The circle of friends who've answered our prayer for help, that is our miracle."

—*Maureen O'Connor Hayden*

Saint Blanche

Back in my cash-poor student-teaching days, I waited tables at a local diner at night to make ends meet. It was a down-home, mom-and-pop operation that specialized in blue plate specials like ham steak and home-made mashed potatoes, real rice pudding, and sweetened iced tea. It was there that I met my first live saint.

Blanche was a wiry, fiery Italian broad with dyed black hair. She drove an old, wheezing, rusted-out station wagon. I never knew her last name, but like Evita or Diana or Oprah, she seemed deserving to be known by one name. Blanche never called in sick. She had more loyal customers than McDonald's. And she had more energy in her fifty-eighth year than I had then or ever in my youth.

At twenty-three, I'd drag myself in after a day of interning, barely able to pour myself a cup of free coffee, and she'd be cleaning out the mayonnaise containers, marrying the ketchup bottles, and filling everybody else's salt and pepper shakers. Not only did she put in six nights a week at the diner, she also spent five days a week as a full-time teacher's aide at a local elementary school.

Blanche wasn't any old teacher's aide, either. She worked in a special-education program that taught physically and developmentally challenged children reading, writing, and arithmetic as well as how to do such things as, oh, walk, and speak through a computer keyboard, and eat. She loved every minute of it and every one of her students. She gave them all nicknames and talked constantly and lovingly about them as if they were her own children:

"PJ finally fed himself a few bites of strained peas today," she would brag about a sixth grader who'd been strapped into the same wheelchair since he was five.

"Rabbit is really starting to get the hang of her new prosthesis," she would report, smiling proudly.

Her joyful recounting of their accomplishments would instantly halt any complaints I'd been preparing to blurt out about my internship at a "normal" junior high school. Eyes bugged and jaw dropped, I'd simply stare at her in silent wonder.

Not once did I hear her complain. As a matter of fact, she rarely uttered a negative word about anything. She never snapped at me for stealing a monkey dish of mashed potatoes or buttered carrots from one of her orders in the kitchen window. And she never hesitated to take an extra table if one of us was "in the weeds" and needed a little help.

After my internship ended and I graduated, I got a real teaching job and stopped working at the diner. I kept meaning to stop by to check on Blanche. But lesson plans and grading and coaching duties kept me busy. Before I knew it, the number of "years taught" on my paycheck stub read five.

That same year I began to seriously wonder whether I'd make it to my sixth year of teaching. I had started out so fresh and new—making up my own quizzes; spending a load of my own money on gifts and prizes, professional resource books, and holiday presents to show the kids I loved them; spending every waking hour thinking up new and creative lesson plans. To avoid the typical grousing and complaining in the faculty lounge, I even ate lunch in my classroom.

I taught at a rough school in a rough neighborhood, and the transition had been difficult. Nevertheless, I thought I'd managed it professionally and knew that I'd welcomed each child into my classroom with an open mind, open heart, and open arms. Unfortunately, some of the more jaded teachers at my grade level quickly noticed and took advantage of my "nurturing" approach, transferring their most troubled students into my room.

Meanwhile, for every troubled student the administration put into my class, they took out a gifted or honor-roll student. Soon my gleaming, vibrantly colored room more closely resembled a set from the film *Dangerous Minds* than from the television show *The Electric Company*. Students stole pencils, defaced posters, and wrote on desks, and I spent more time filling out detention slips and discipline referrals than I did making lesson plans and grading papers. Before long, I became the loudest complainer in the faculty lounge I'd once avoided.

As my fifth year of teaching progressed, I grew increasingly more tired, frustrated, angry, and disappointed. I dreaded the weekdays, because they meant an eight-hour

struggle followed by several more hours of parent confer-
ences, expulsion meetings, and detentions. I dreaded the
weekends, because they flew by too quickly and meant yet
another week was just around the corner. Though it pained
me to admit it, I was burnt out. I'd had enough. I'd even
started to check the want ads every Sunday and to speak
with old college buddies about jobs in their gleaming, high-
rise office buildings.

Then one night on my way home from work, I stopped
into a new Italian restaurant for some takeout. On my way
out, just before the door closed behind me, I heard
Blanche's unmistakable voice calling to me from behind
the cash register. As we hugged and reminisced, I noticed
that, although her black hair wasn't quite so black anymore, her love for her students hadn't dimmed one bit.

When I asked about her class that year, she didn't miss
a beat in telling me all about her new bunch of "great
kids"—how "Shorty has finally gotten used to his new
feeding tube" and that "JR is taking an experimental
seizure medication." I decided to dine in and sit at one of
her tables so we could visit a bit more.

Although it had been another long day for me, I knew
it had been an even longer one for Blanche. Yet, as she
spoke enthusiastically about her kids, it occurred to me
that no matter what challenges and struggles she went
through, she continued to hang in there and give it her
all, day by day, year after year. None of those kids would
ever forget Blanche, just as I would never forget her.

As I sat there in that vinyl booth listening to her crusty
voice speaking eloquently of sacrifice and duty, of honesty

and love, a weight lifted from my shoulders and the haze cleared from my vision. If Blanche could muster up the energy and will every day to give to others who needed it so desperately, then I could dig in my feet and find a better way to get through to my students. After all, I hadn't gone into teaching because it was lucrative, glamorous, or an easy ride. I'd become a teacher, I suddenly realized, to become like Blanche—a glimmer of hope in a young person's heart, someone he or she could look up to, someone to help guide him or her toward a better tomorrow.

When it came time to pay the bill, long after I'd finished my dinner but not long enough for Blanche and me to catch up on five years of living and teaching, I emptied my wallet to leave her the biggest tip I could. I knew it could never be enough to repay her. I also knew that I was the one who was leaving the richer, secure in my resolution to remain a teacher.

—*Rusty Fischer*

True Love in Action

When I moved to Australia from New Zealand twelve years ago, I knew only one person—Shirley. She and her husband and two small babies opened their doors and hearts wide to me. For the next six months while I got settled into the big, bustling city of Sydney, I took over their sunroom. I became their boarder, and they became my surrogate family. In the ensuing years, Shirley has always been there for me, offering a home to return to and a friend to turn to.

To know Shirley is to love Shirley. Her legion of friends is testimony to that. She often jokes that she could never get up to mischief, because wherever she goes, even to the most remote or nondescript places, she always seems to bump into a friend or friendly acquaintance. Her soul is an open book, and what others inevitably find there are generosity, compassion, wisdom, good humor, and comfort. That she has worked for many years in a helping profession, as a nurse, just seems to fit, and she brings the same magical combination of caring, attention, and humor to her job as she does to her friends. A gracious hostess and an attentive listener, she's as apt to give you the shirt off her back as she is to give you a gentle, well-needed kick in the pants. She can engage in meaningful conversations for hours on end and just as easily have you rolling with laughter. She can hobnob with the rich and famous just as easily as she can open her heart and lend a hand to the homeless and heartbroken. And she has done both.

One of Shirley's most remarkable qualities is her understanding and nurturing of the downtrodden. Perhaps it is because she is so well acquainted with grief that she is able to empathize with others who are struggling and suffering. When she was ten years old, her father committed suicide. It was Shirley who found him. That horrific fact is not what she holds in her mind and heart; it is the loss of a beloved father who was also her best friend. Tragedy struck again when, six weeks before her wedding, her fiancé died suddenly of a heart attack. Over the years, like most of us, Shirley has had an ample share of trials and sorrows. Yet, she never lets her own circumstances or struggles prevent her from reaching out to others—including me.

In all the ups and downs, dramas and demands of my life, Shirley has been a comforting constant. When I need her, even when I don't realize I need her, she's always there to lift my spirits and to help ease my load, while never passing judgment or doling out recriminations.

"Be gentle on yourself, Marcie," she has often said, or, "We're all human. We all make mistakes."

Not that she sees human frailty as an excuse for failure or that she is a passive people pleaser; quite the contrary.

This is a woman of principle who is not afraid to speak out, whether by writing a letter to a lawmaker or newspaper about some injustice or by challenging a butcher in his crowded shop about his unethical dealings. Shirley has the ability to speak up for her convictions in a way that is at once candid yet calm, pointed yet polite. Our only falling out, of sorts, was when she challenged me (nicely, of course) about my selfishness during one period in my life. I love and respect her for doing that, because her loving reprimand shook me from my self-absorption.

She came through again when I was struggling to break away from a rigid fundamentalist religious group that had isolated me from loved ones and driven me from a loving relationship with God. Shirley gently pushed through that religion of hate and lent a guiding hand as I struggled to establish a new, healthier spirituality.

Then, during that difficult period, I got pregnant. I was mortified, filled with fear and guilt, and I felt completely alone. For a while, I told no one, fearing the judgment of my Christian friends and family. Finally, I turned to the one person I knew I could count on: Shirley.

"Marcie, these things happen. We're all human," she said when I told her. "It doesn't make you a bad person. It doesn't lessen God's love for you, or mine."

When I miscarried, it was Shirley who drove me home from the hospital and who comforted me with her usual compassion and care.

Years later, Shirley again offered her unconditional love and support, during my new husband's heroin addiction. Even when she expressed her concerns and misgivings about me staying in the marriage and questioned my husband's desire and ability to overcome his addiction, she never judged me or him. And she never again questioned my decision to be with him. While my relationships with family and other friends, who naturally did not understand my husband's illness or my decision to stay with him, grew strained and distant, Shirley remained a soothing presence in my life. What's more, she extended the same compassion toward my husband. Whenever she saw him, her queries as to his well-being were warm and genuine.

After my husband nearly overdosed, it was Shirley I called from the emergency room. Because we were in the process of moving to another state and had already moved out of our home, we stayed with Shirley while he recovered. By then, my husband had been struggling with his drug addiction for more than four years, and most of our family and friends had given up on him. Not Shirley. She took him for a walk the morning after the overdose and encouraged him not to give up. "We're all human," she said. "We all slide down the slippery slope sometimes." And it was Shirley who celebrated his hard-won victory over heroin addiction with us.

My friend Shirley demonstrates through her words and deeds a true understanding and love of humanity—a belief that we are all fallible and all loveable. Someone once said to me: "Human love is loving because of something; divine love is loving in spite of everything." Shirley is the epitome of true love in action.

—Marcia Tibbo

I'll Give You a Dime

My cousin Lita and I were born in 1944, only three and a half months apart, the daughters of two close sisters. While Lita's father served in the Army, she and her mother moved in with us for a while. Our mothers often put us together in the same crib, and we grew up feeling more like twin sisters than cousins. From infancy, Lita was my closest friend and a mirror to my soul. Although they moved out when her father returned from the war, Lita and her family stayed in the same city as ours, and our mothers visited each other often. So, we spent a great deal of time together. We confided in each other, divulged our dreams, and shared many of the same interests.

When we were old enough, we would spend the night at each other's house almost every weekend, well into junior high school. We might have continued the arrangement, but something even better happened. My parents moved into a house that was connected to Lita's by a short pathway through a patch of woods. At last we could see each other every day. We wore the trail down raw, crossing back and forth between our houses. We also walked to school and home together five days a week.

Our friendship wasn't always simple and carefree. Like siblings, we had spats once in a while. I can barely recall the reasons for any of our tiffs, because the outcome never changed; we always found ourselves drawn together again. The invisible thread that bound us might have frayed from time to time, but it never broke. I think we began to respect and understand that bond when we were both about seven years old—when we had one skirmish neither of us ever forgot. It put our relationship in perspective and securely tied us together for life.

Here is what happened: On one of her many visits, Lita brought over a comic book to read. We were both avid readers of anything, and comic books represented a special treat. At the time, the flimsy books cost a whopping ten cents. We could have gotten two ice cream cones—one for each of us—for that amount of money.

When Lita finished reading the comic book, she said I could read it, too, and handed it to me. I sat cross-legged on the floor of my bedroom and soon grew immersed in the stories. She tried to talk to me several times, but lost in a fantasy world, I ignored her. Archie comics were my favorite, after all. I never cared for the silly talking duck stuff, but teens doing things I longed to do one day fascinated me. Instantly, the book wove its magic on me. I laughed at the goofy parts, sighed at the slightly romantic parts, and dreamed of the day I might be a teen myself. Betty and Veronica even had a relationship much like my friendship with Lita. I slid into the world of the stories and forgot all about reality.

Lita hung around a short time, but finally, bored out of her wits, she left to do something else. I hardly noticed her absence.

At the end of the comic book, I found a Veronica paper doll, complete with several bright changes of clothing, garments I would have loved to own. The doll had a figure I would have loved to own, too. Without another thought, I reached for my scissors and merrily cut along the dotted lines, eager to see how Veronica looked in each of her spiffy outfits.

Lita stepped back into the room and cried out, "What are you doing?"

I stopped mid-snip and snapped back to reality. The book wasn't mine, and I had totally forgotten. Humiliated, I tried to explain my inexcusable lapse.

She threw up her hands and stormed from the room, refusing to speak to me.

I felt crushed and embarrassed. How could I have forgotten that the book was hers, not mine? Alone in my room, angry with myself and frustrated that I could not appease my best friend, I cried. Several times I left my room to find her, but she sat at the bottom of the stairs, brooding, and shunned me. She wouldn't even acknowledge my apologies.

Her mother arrived to take her home, and I knew I had only a few more minutes to make peace before they left. While my mother and hers sat and talked, I desperately dug into a drawer and found my piggy bank. I squinted through its pink, knobby glass at the few coins inside, to make sure I had what I needed, then I dashed downstairs and past Lita, who sat in preparation to leave. I hurried into the kitchen, opened a drawer, pulled out a butter knife, slipped the flat edge into the piggy bank slot, and jiggled and manipulated the meager contents until I finally withdrew the right amount of money. I ran from the kitchen and hurried back to the steps, only to find Lita still fuming, still sitting on a bottom stair, still waiting to go home.

I held out my shiny coin. "You can buy another comic book. Please don't be angry at me."

She would not look at me, so I stepped around to her other side and held out the peace offering again. "I'm sorry," I said. "I'll give you a dime."

Lita glanced at the ten-cent piece in my hand and looked up at my face, which was hot from embarrassment and wet with tears. She sighed, and her expression softened. "That's okay," she said. "I know you didn't mean it."

In that instant, our friendship deepened, as we both realized our friendship was much more valuable than a measly comic book. We hugged and ran off to play together again for the few minutes we had left before Aunt Anita took Lita home.

Life went on—about fifty more years of it. We went through high school and part of college together. As young adults, we both moved to Orlando, Florida, for a while, but I moved back home and then to Baltimore, Maryland.

Lita and I have lived in separate cities now for about thirty-six years, yet we remain close friends to this day. Like sisters, we still have similar interests, and we still squabble from time to time. We always make up, though, sometimes with a phone call that begins, "I'll give you a dime . . ."

—*Bobbie Christmas*

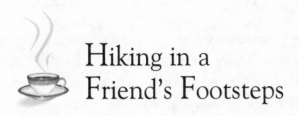

Hiking in a Friend's Footsteps

F or most Florida suburbanites, the word *hike* means the long trek from the car to the mall when the parking lot is crowded. At least, that's what I always thought it meant—until about eighteen years ago when I moved to the mountains of North Georgia and took my first real hike. One needs an experienced guide for such adventures. Enter Thelma Bennett, a.k.a. "Tommy," well known throughout Georgia and North Carolina as the "Ole Woman of the Mountains." It is a moniker well earned: This little lady knows most of the wildflowers and terrain in the area, and has probably hiked nearly all of it. By day's end, I was impressed by her knowledge of the myriad flora and fauna we encountered and even more so by her incredible stamina.

When I first met Tommy, I remember thinking that, at age sixty-two, she seemed pretty old to be hiking. I was then in my mid-forties, and I was expecting to seek more sedentary activities by the time I reached her age. In the eighteen years since my first hike with Tommy, she has altered my thinking on that and scores of other subjects.

I soon discovered that her age had no impact on many of

her pursuits and certainly not on her taste for adventure. Neither did her diminutive size. Though she has to look through the steering wheel of the car, she drives like a racecar driver, and the sharply twisting mountain curves are her forte.

Tommy and I are friends, but we are not equally yoked. Despite our age difference being almost that of mother and daughter, she can out-hike me going backward on any given day. Sometimes she doesn't invite me to go on certain hikes, because, quite frankly, they are too difficult for me. Mostly, though, she adjusts her pace to include me in some wondrous adventures. Over the years, Tommy introduced me to more than a dozen fascinating trails, with names like Standing Indian, Brasstown Bald, Chunky Gal Gap, Tate City, and Raven's Cliff. I will forever cherish our memorable walk through Noland's Creek amidst the most beautiful autumn foliage I've ever seen. We have hiked in heat, in rain, and in cold, and we have slogged through oozing red Georgia mud. Each experience has invariably created an incalculable memory for me.

While we hiked and walked, and when we stopped to take in a breathtaking vista or for a picnic lunch next to a babbling brook, Tommy talked with me, and she listened to me. She took me under her wing and showed me how to respect and revel in the wonder of creation. She has taught me what to look for and what to watch out for, how to still the beating of my anxious heart as I face new experiences, and how to be grateful for the experience. In turn, I grew in experience, wisdom, and grace. In fact, I grew up a lot under her tutelage.

Tommy helped me sort out my understanding of relationships with growing and grown children. She encouraged me to begin a unique quilting venture, which other people, including a well-respected quilt judge, summarily dismissed. When I felt compelled to write an inspirational book but doubted my abilities and qualifications to do it, Tommy pooh-poohed the notion that having never written a book meant I couldn't and shouldn't. My quilting business now takes me on travels throughout the country, and that book is now in its third printing. So, not only has Tommy been my hiking guide and friend, she's also been my mentor.

Once while hiking, when I was feeling tired and sore, I asked Tommy if she ever experienced pain when she hiked.

"Why, my dear," she replied. "Of course! I hurt every day of my life, but I just keep on going."

Now nearly eighty, despite numerous ailments, surgeries, and injuries, Tommy continues to embody her belief that life is to be filled with faith and perseverance.

For my sixty-second birthday, Tommy made reservations for the two of us at the Len Foote Hike Inn. The celebration included a five-mile hike (the only way to reach the inn), dinner, an overnight stay in clean but rustic accommodations, a hearty breakfast the next morning, and the five-mile return hike. Eighteen years ago, if anyone had asked me how I expected to celebrate my sixty-second year, the farthest thing from my mind would have been a ten-mile hike! But Tommy reminds me not to get mired down in thinking of age as a self-limiting number, and she prods me to see myself as able and capable.

On our Hike-Inn trek, we walked through awesome banks of fog and mist, and at times through drenching rain. I pressed my ninety-nine-cent bright orange fold-up rain poncho into service, but the rain never dampened my spirits. We came upon a pileated woodpecker, spooked a couple of wild turkeys into flight, saw evidence of a bear having over-turned some stumps looking for grubs, and beheld wondrous specimens of mushrooms, lichen, and moss. Stands of rhododendron and mountain laurel surrounded us, along with blankets of dainty maidenhair fern, which contrasted with massive trees of every variety. A mysterious, indescrib-able hush filled the air—a sentient silence that invited deep thought and reflection.

The next morning, I was only one day older, but I felt infinitely wiser. My mirror seemed to reflect a woman ten feet tall—wearing a silly grin on her face! Nothing compares with a hike in the woods. It brings restoration and renewal, serenity, and a quiet communion with God. The experience is even more rewarding when shared with a friend.

A day spent in the woods, or anywhere, with a willing mentor is truly a gift. Over the years, Tommy's willingness to accept this role in my life has made me more willing to pass along the gift of such a relationship to others. As a conse-quence, I've offered my home and my time to a few young mothers who have found in me an open and agreeable ear as they work through their challenges. If I can pass along to them even half the wisdom and joy that Tommy has given me, I will be grateful. Perhaps one day, when one of them lacks sufficient faith in herself, I'll treat her to a ten-mile hike in the forest.

For now, having just come down yet another moun-tain with my hiking friend of more than eighteen years, it is enough to simply accept the gift of the experience, and of Tommy, with awe and thanksgiving.

—*Arlene M. Gray*

A Song in My Heart

Every day as I walked home from elementary school I saw him sitting in the shade of his garage reading the paper. Although we never spoke and never so much as waved to each other, I began to view this older man as a friend of sorts.

Growing up in the 1970s, I suppose I was less cautious than children might be these days. But this man lived in a charming, immaculately kept home in my own neighborhood. He had a balding head and a kind face, and he wore cardigan sweaters on cool days and reading spectacles. To me, he looked like the perfect grandfather. I noticed that he left every day around dinnertime and was always gone all day on Sunday. I fancied that he visited his grandchildren during those times and entertained them with his jokes, perhaps bounced a little one on his knee and was mobbed with hugs as he attempted to leave their homes each time. I smiled to myself as I imagined the scene.

One day on my walk home from school, the man wasn't out there in his garage reading the paper like he was supposed to be. The whole rest of that day felt wrong to me, but I couldn't quite pinpoint why. What did it matter to me whether I saw an old man reading his paper or not? Yet, somehow it did.

The next day I was again disappointed to find that my friend was not reading outside as I'd hoped he'd be. Being an outgoing and determined child, I marched myself over to his house to find out exactly why.

I knocked on the front door once, twice, and then heard the sound of someone coming to the door. Now, it hadn't occurred to me that it might be bad manners to just drop in on someone I didn't really know. To my thinking, I was perfectly within my rights to ask why he wasn't out there as usual.

The elderly man, clad in a red plaid flannel robe and striped pajamas, opened the door. I'd obviously awakened him from a nap, and I was mortified to find that his reason for not being outside was that he was sick in bed. With my cheeks flaming, I hastily introduced myself and apologized for being upset with him for not being outside reading like he was supposed to be. Humor crept into his eyes, and a warm smile quickly replaced his baffled expression. He introduced himself as Carl Vrem and said that he hoped he would feel well enough to be outside tomorrow so as not to disappoint me. I flushed with embarrassment, and as he laughed, the nicest crinkles formed around his eyes. He said, "You know, it was worth getting sick to actually meet you, Miss Wendy. You're quite a character. Come on over anytime and cheer me up." So I did—about an hour later.

First, though, I rushed home, bursting into my parents' kitchen with the announcement that one of my best friends was very sick. My mother, who was in the middle of some household project, expressed sympathy. When I told her I wanted to take my friend some chicken soup and orange juice to help him get well, she asked, "Wendy, why doesn't your friend's parents take care of him?" I soberly told her that I thought they were dead. Distracted by her project, she gave me permission to take my get-well offering to my friend, as long as I didn't stay too long or make a pest of myself.

I ran all the way to Mr. Vrem's house, knocked on the door again, and presented my offering of soup, juice, and some muffins I'd quickly made from a mix. He thanked me profusely, and I felt so happy at being able to help my new friend.

The next day Mr. Vrem was outside as usual, and I stopped by to ask how he was feeling. He assured me that he felt much better and thanked me for my concern. He asked me what grade I was in and about my family, and he told me that he was a retired pharmacist and had raised his children in this very home. Being the cheeky thing I was, I asked him if that's where he went each night and on Sundays, to see his children and grandchildren.

Laughing, he said, "No, I have no grandchildren, and my children live far away. I don't care much for cooking, so I usually eat out each night and then stop by to see my wife, Jeanne, in the care home where she lives. I also visit her on Sundays and during the day while you're at school."

Before I could ask him why his wife didn't live at home, he sadly told me she'd always been a delicate woman, and her bones had become so fragile that any fall or injury caused them to break. He looked down sorrowfully as he told me that he had tried to take care of her himself, but several years earlier, she had taken a bad fall and broken several bones while he was mowing the lawn. He showed me pictures of his wife, and she had been a lovely woman. She reminded me of Audrey Hepburn. He also showed me pictures of his son and daughter who lived back East. He told me how he had worked two jobs to pay for them to go to Ivy League schools. He was very proud of them.

The next day I went by Mr. Vrem's house with a picture of some flowers I had drawn for his wife. He was delighted and took them to her that evening when he took her laundry to her. This sweet man would handwash his wife's delicate clothing and hang it to dry, because she didn't want strangers handling her clothing and possibly ruining it. I thought, how wonderful it would be to marry a man who was kind enough to handwash your dainties just because it made you happy. As nice as my father was, I could never see him doing such a thing. In fact, my dad always chose long flannel nightgowns when he shopped for my mother. My friend Mr. Vrem had the right idea about how to treat a woman.

On some days after I had visited with Mr. Vrem, my mother would ask why I was so late getting home from school. I'd tell her, "Oh, I was just talking with my friend." Never in her wildest dreams did my mother imagine who my friend was. You can imagine her surprise, then, when he showed up at our house at Christmastime with a huge gift for our family. My mother stammered and finally asked him, "You're Wendy's friend?" Chuckling, he said, "I certainly am. That's quite a daughter you've got there!"

Afterward, my mother admonished me not to bother

that nice man too much. So, I walked over and asked him, "Do I bother you, Mr. Vrem?" He laughed and said, "Heavens no! I don't know what I'd do without you. Please don't stop coming over, singing songs for me, telling me about your life, and making my days so bright." I looked at him seriously. Then I grinned, extended my hand as though we were conducting an important business transaction, and replied, "Okay, it's a deal!"

Things went on like that for a few years. I'd stop by and visit after school and during vacations and summers. We shared Coca-Colas together on his back porch, and he explained the difference between gram-negative and gram-positive bacteria and the usefulness of various antibiotics against each. I soaked up the information and his attention like a sponge, and decided that there had never been anyone quite as wonderful as Mr. Vrem.

I loved to sing and was practicing for a Christmas program one evening at the choir director's home when the phone rang. It was my oldest brother, wanting to talk to me. Paul told me that while he had been working at the steakhouse, Carl Vrem had come in for dinner. So? I wondered. Mr. Vrem ate out a lot; why was my brother calling me at someone else's house to tell me that? Paul cleared his throat and continued gently, "Sis, while he was eating, they think he had a stroke, and he had to be taken to the hospital. They're not sure whether he's going to make it." I heard the sounds of an anguished animal wailing with pain, and I threw down the phone and locked myself in the bathroom, sobbing. It wasn't until later that I realized I had been the source of that horrible crying.

When Mr. Vrem was well enough for visitors, my parents took me to the hospital to see him. He was thin and white, and his left side was paralyzed. I tried not to notice his clownlike expressions as he tried to speak to me. He was barely holding on to life and could hardly speak. He cried as he tried over and over to tell me something, but I had trouble understanding him. Finally, I realized that the garbled words he was trying to say were, "I love you."

I cried and held his hand as I told him, "I love you, too. You're my best friend." I didn't know what else to say, yet I didn't want to leave him. So, I decided to sing for him. Holding that dear man's hand in mine, I sang every Christmas carol I knew. When I began to sing "Silent Night," he finally closed his eyes. And as I sang the words, "Sleep in heavenly peace," he did.

—*Wendy Marvel Redmond*

After the Heartache

"It's over," I said. "I'm coming back to Iowa. Can I stay with you?"

"Of course," you said.

"It" was the longest relationship of my life, a profound but tumultuous love affair with Sarah, whom I had met five years earlier during my graduate program at the University of Iowa and two years later had followed to North Carolina.

"You" was not one person, but several—my friends back home in Iowa.

After months of trying to hold things together, Sarah had finally kicked me out at the start of her Thanksgiving break. She asked me to have everything out of the house we'd bought together by the time she got back. I was wracked with grief and exhausted from months of turmoil. I'd never fought so hard for anything in my life, and I still didn't know why we'd failed, why I'd failed. I'd been working on the dissertation, or trying to, for a year. With each passing month, Sarah and I had spent more and more hours late at night trying to revive our love, succeeding only in tiring ourselves out. As our relationship fell apart, my dissertation had fallen to the wayside. The only thing I could think to do was go back to Iowa to lick my wounds and finish my turmoil-delayed dissertation.

I called my friends in Iowa—the same ones I had neglected, almost forgotten, as I fought to keep love alive. I packed everything I owned in three days, crying most of the time. When I wasn't crying, I was phoning my friends in Iowa: Heidi, Ray, Teri, Rob, Michelle.

Most of them had been concerned about my move to North Carolina three years earlier. Though they were all for love and couldn't have been more supportive in that regard, they had pointed out that 50 percent of graduate students who leave campus don't finish their dissertations.

"Are you sure you want to do this?" they had asked.

When I assured them that I did, they had accepted my decision without criticism or further questioning. They expressed their confidence in me and helped me make the arrangements to complete the doctorate from a distance.

When it all fell apart, they stepped forward to help me close that distance, again without question or criticism. Not one of them said, "I told you so," even though I'd fretted to them frequently about the lack of progress on my dissertation. None of them said, "You should have seen this coming," even though they'd suffered through my frequent and depressing calls about my failing relationship. Nor did they judge or hedge when I asked for their help.

Heidi, who had recently gone through a rugged divorce and was living in a small apartment, asked only, "Do you think you'll have enough room here to work?"

Ray, who had also gone through a hard breakup and

had no extra living space, said simply, "Come on."

My dissertation advisor, Rob, the only man I know who owns more books than I do, willingly took in the sixty boxes of books I mailed to him. He brushed the snow off the cartons and piled them in his living room, where they filled one entire half of the room.

I packed my car to the brim with memories I had been too tired to organize, and headed home. I wept during the long drive from North Carolina to Iowa. I wept at night in lonely motels in the Smoky Mountains and in Illinois. I didn't weep at meals, and considered that a victory. I arrived in Iowa City the day after Thanksgiving in the midst of an ice storm—cold, red-eyed, and empty-hearted.

My friends took me in, opening their homes and their hearts. Iowa City is a university town, and since school was in session, housing was in short supply. It took more than seventy phone calls to find an apartment. Ray fielded all the return calls and was a constant source of practical and moral support. He and Heidi took turns housing and humoring me. Rob held on to my books for the many weeks it took me to find my own place. He, Teri, and Michelle helped me lug those sixty boxes of books up two flights of stairs when I finally found a tiny, drafty apartment, made all the more desolate by its utter emptiness.

I had no furniture, having left it all in North Carolina, so that Sarah and her daughter would have places to sit, eat, and sleep. And I had no money to furnish the place. I sat alone on the floor, futilely trying to push away my grief and to write the dissertation on my laptop. That lasted a day, until Rob showed up with some tables, lamps, and dishes, and offered chairs and rugs. He claimed I was doing him a favor by getting them out of the way. Right.

Then, one by one, my friends would "just happen by" at dinnertime. They'd call, just to say "Hi" or under the innocuous claim of needing to talk over some teaching challenge. Videos were loaned, invitations were extended, and everyone put up with what was essentially a corpse at the feast, still picking at the scabs of a relationship.

One day over lunch and small talk, Rob, my advisor, suddenly changed the subject and commented on how little work the most recent chapter of my dissertation needed. I hadn't worked on the dissertation for months and couldn't imagine this was true. Just to prove him wrong, I dug the chapter out of a box and started reviewing Rob's advisory notes and suggested changes. A few hours later, I realized I'd done the first productive thing for myself since I'd returned to Iowa. Then, since the boxes were already open, I put a few things on the shelves and began the slow transition from man-living-in-cave-with-boxes to normal human being.

My friends continued to nurture me back to life. No one said they were trying to help me feel better. No one even implied I needed help, emotional cripple that I was. I didn't have the energy to figure out or do the things I needed to do to get my life back together. I didn't have to. My friends did.

Heidi never asked how I was doing in getting over Sarah; neither did Teri. Instead, both of them shared snippets of their recent divorces over coffee, admitting how hard it had been, but accenting the fact that they'd gotten through it. Michelle listened to my endless self-analyses, never arguing and only occasionally redirecting my blame into examination and my excavation of the past into a lesson for the future.

On New Year's Eve, after only six weeks under the care and counsel of my friends, I was standing with Rob and Ray on frosted grass alongside the Iowa River after an evening of too much pizza and hysterical laughter. At midnight, the fireworks exploded in the sky, joined by the icy puffs of our breath as we watched in blessed silence and companionship. In that moment, I knew everything would be all right.

By the end of that new year, I had finished my dissertation. A year later, I was dating someone new, the wonderful Kathleen. I was whole and happy again—because my friends had caught me when I'd shattered and held the pieces of my soul and my life together while I'd healed.

—*Greg Beatty*

Breaking the Silence

Silence. Silence so deafening my head ached from it. No laughter, no cries, no voices came from the hall into the stillness of the private room at the end of a long corridor in the surgical wing.

Just hours before the room had vibrated with the sounds of nurses, beeping machines, and shouted instructions. This silent room was my final, unexpected destination after two days in a labor-and-delivery room in the maternity wing, where I'd grown accustomed to the hustle and bustle of welcoming new life into the world. I heard mothers screaming with pain, crying with joy, and laughing with delight at first sight of their newborns. Now, there was nothing but emptiness and silence.

As I lay in my hospital bed, staring blindly out the window, I couldn't believe the world was actually continuing. I watched the construction crews, the people driving by, the comings and goings of the hospital workers and visitors, wondering how it was that their lives hadn't come to a screeching halt as mine had. How could life go on when the lives of my babies, who were stillborn at twenty-two weeks, had ended before my babies could take their first breaths? How could I go on without them?

It was bad enough that strangers and the hospital staff were oblivious to my pain. That my loved ones seemed unable to face my joy in my babies' existence and my sorrow at their loss was unbearable. For months, the anticipation of having identical twin girls running around was all anyone could talk about. Suddenly now, when I so desperately needed to share my thoughts, love, hopes, and memories of them, the topic was taboo. Family and friends came, and I know they, too, were grieving for the babies. Yet, no one said a word about my first-borns. Any attempt I made to talk about the babies was greeted with steer-her-away-from-there comments—or silence.

One day I overheard the nurse talking to my parents and husband in the hallway. "She needs closure. You'll have to help her let go of them."

"How?" my mother asked.

"Encourage her to get on with her life and to put this behind her. Go pack up all the baby things, so she won't have to go through the pain of doing it when she goes home," the nurse said. "And don't discuss the babies."

I pictured the two matching outfits with teddy bears stitched on the pockets that I had bought the week before and began to cry at the thought of someone putting them in a box. Sadness turned into silent anger. When my husband and parents entered the room, I continued to look out the window and met their greetings with silence. Then I turned and said, "Despite any advice you've been given, do not touch anything in the nursery. Do not even open the door. If I go home and find one thing out of place, I will never forgive you for it."

Speechless, they simply nodded, sat down, and proceeded to follow the nurse's other advice, making no mention of the babies.

When I dared to bring them up, the conversation would immediately turn to something else. Even my father, who normally lingers on crisis-at-hand issues, changed the subject when I mentioned the babies.

"For identical twins, they didn't look a thing alike," I said. "I think they both looked like Mom, though."

"Yeah, you're right. . . . I wonder what they're planning to do with all that fill dirt piled up out there," he said, looking out the window.

After a while, I gave up. And the room fell silent.

By afternoon, I was exhausted from the silence, from everyone trying so hard to forget what I wanted so much to remember. So I decided to remember them alone and asked that no more visitors be allowed into the room.

That evening as darkness fell, there was a knock on the door. My husband came in to say that his family had been waiting for hours and would like to know if they could see me now.

"No," I said quietly.

"Christa's here."

My heart warmed a little. I'd always loved Christa, my husband's sister, as a friend and as the sister I'd never had. I realized I wanted to see her, and I didn't want to leave out or alienate my other in-laws, so I agreed to see them all for a short visit.

They filed into the room—my husband's parents, his younger sister, Christa, and her husband. Everyone huddled around my bed except for Christa. She leaned against the wall as if patiently waiting for her turn to speak. After all the

"It's okay, they are with God now" and "The doctor said you can have more children" comments were spoken, silence again filled the room, and everyone left but Christa.

She walked over and sat down on the chair beside my bed. She took her wallet from her purse and removed a small, folded piece of paper from underneath her driver's license. She unfolded it carefully, gently ran her fingers over it, and with a warm smile placed it in my hand. I looked down and saw a photocopy of two tiny footprints.

"Here are my babies," she said. "Now, tell me about yours."

Suddenly I remembered that Christa, too, had lost twin daughters, stillborn at twenty-three weeks. She knew the silence of my grief was drowning me, and she threw me a lifeline.

Friendship is doing what you know is best for your friend, even if it goes against popular opinion. Christa knew I longed for the lives of those babies and that their death would not stop that longing. She knew that although I had carried them for only a few months, I felt close to them. She knew that not remembering them would further wound, rather than heal, me.

So, we talked and cried, we talked and smiled, and we talked some more. We talked about our children's beautiful little faces and how the muscles on their legs looked so strong. We talked about how we knew they would have grown into doctors, lawyers, writers, Nobel Prize winners, or great moms. It didn't really matter what dreams we held for them; all that mattered was that we had dreams for them. We talked about how special they were, how terribly we missed them, and how much we loved them and would always love them.

Finally, the silence was broken.

—*Sylvia E. Sheets McDonald*

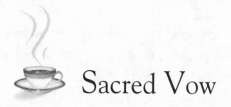

Sacred Vow

The new millennium did not bring the apocalypse that some thought it would. What it did bring for me, however, was a new appreciation for my dear friend of thirty-five years, Mary. Perhaps it was Mary's extended visit with her sister that made me realize how much our daily conversations brightened my day and what a void her absence created. Maybe it was losing too many friends before I had let them know I was thankful our paths had crossed that made me determined not to take my friendship with Mary for granted. Perhaps it was a milestone birthday lurking around the corner for each of us—my seventieth, her seventy-fifth—that made me reflect on what a blessing she has been in my life.

An only child, I've always thought of Mary as the sister I would have chosen had that been possible. At one time, we actually were related, through the marriage of my daughter and her son. Had our children not fallen in love, Mary and I might never have met. Then again, I don't believe in coincidence. Though our children brought us together, fate made us friends.

Shortly after our children started dating, Mary invited me to join in a garage sale that she and a few neighbors were planning. Being a newcomer to Houston, I was delighted with the invitation. As we worked together, I discovered that Mary was an amazing organizer. She was also plainspoken and didn't gossip. We ended up with coins jingling in our pockets and the beginning of a great friendship.

By the time the children asked for our blessings on their marriage, we were woven into the fabric of one another's lives. Mary used her creative talents to make my daughter's wedding dress, consulting and fitting until the bride-to-be spun around the room in breathless delight. My assignment was the veil, which I adorned with tiny seed pearls and bugle beads. Wearing the bridal ensemble created by her two moms, "our" twenty-year-old daughter made a beautiful bride to "our" handsome twenty-year-old son.

When the marriage unraveled three years later, both families were devastated. But neither Mary nor I blamed or withheld our love from either of our children. Nor did we allow their decision to drive a wedge between us. They divorced. We did not.

The bond between us had been forged long before our children's estrangement, even before their engagement. I first recognized it one night as we hung wallpaper. I have to admit that I doubted Mary's sanity when she showed up to help me wallpaper a few rooms and then stayed to work until the wee hours of the morning. We could've plastered ourselves to the wall with the stray paste. What sticks in my mind, aside from our laughter and camaraderie, was the unspoken understanding that passed between us—

that we'd always be there for each other. We were too naive then to realize the importance that silent vow would hold in later years.

Outsiders would probably think it unlikely that two such different people could be such grand friends. Mary and I are opposites in many ways. I thrive on chaos; she's a neat freak. I've yet to meet a stranger; she is reserved. I'm an animal lover, any animal, with two cats. She loves one adorable dog but dislikes all felines, though she's made a concerted effort to befriend my furry companions. These and other differences proved to be minor issues.

Our similar interests and shared values have given us plenty of common ground. We both enjoy creative endeavors, from sewing to writing, and stirring up memorable meals. There was a time when we could've hired out as a pair of gardening experts. Countless times over the years, we'd pull ourselves from our gardens; scrub and repair dirty, broken fingernails; and meet at a favorite restaurant for an evening of good food and better conversation.

At the top of our respective lists of best things in life are family, friends, and fun. I'll never forget the night we left a charity benefit howling with laughter. The look from the valet clearly indicated that he thought we'd hit the wine bottle one too many times. I didn't care what he thought— but I certainly was glad it was Mary, and not he, who saw me stroll out of the restroom with my skirt tucked up in the back of my pantyhose. I still have no idea how I managed to drive while gasping for breath and dabbing at the tears streaming down my face. Every time I quit laughing, Mary would start and get us both going again.

It was the laughter and the easy companionship that I missed most when I moved with my family to Dallas. I made new friends, and Mary and I stayed in touch with cards, phone calls, and occasional visits. But it wasn't the same. I missed Mary's presence in my everyday life.

By the time I moved back to Houston as a divorcee, Mary had lost her beloved husband to cancer. Though our lifestyles had changed dramatically by choice and chance, we gradually picked up where we'd left off. Together we discovered how different, and often painful, it was to tread through uncharted waters as single women in a predominately coupled world. Once we regained our footing, we discovered an even stronger friendship.

The strength of that friendship helped us through the unthinkable: the tragic loss of Mary's sixteen-year-old granddaughter and the disappearance of my son, who has been missing for more than a decade. How easy it would've been to surrender to grief and pain, to isolate in our misery. Instead, we reached out for and comforted one another. The heightened awareness of the uncertain future we all face prompted us to never miss an opportunity to tell family and friends we love them.

Through life's myriad challenges and changes, Mary has been a constant—an endless source of joy and comfort. In turn, there is nothing I wouldn't do for her. That has made these past several years of accompanying her to incessant procedures that have failed to relieve her constant pain all the more difficult to bear.

In spite of her physical discomfort and a lifetime of surgeries, Mary has always kept her sense of humor. Having decided to leave her body to science, she jokes that there'll probably be nothing of value left when her time comes. Her legacy of generosity, however, is invaluable and extends to all who know her. As just one example, when her housekeeper got married, Mary gave the newlyweds an all-expenses-paid weekend at her beachfront condo. Though I've never had the financial means to offer quite so extravagant a gift, I've borrowed a page from Mary's unwritten Instruction Book for Life, giving what I could to others, expecting nothing in return.

Another bit of Mary's wisdom goes like this: When you receive a gift, rather than repaying that person, pass along the kindness by doing something special for someone else. While many folks tout this idiom in theory, Mary has embraced it as a way of life, and I've attempted to do the same.

Still, our differing financial situations caused me to do some soul searching when she offered to treat me to a cruise. After announcing that she wouldn't make the trip alone and it was up to me whether we seized the moment or sat home twiddling our thumbs, the two of us tucked books, swimsuits, and a few fancy rags into our luggage and sailed away. What an incredible experience we shared! And what fun it was to watch the reaction of strangers when they learned of the circumstances of our friendship.

At sea or on the road, I couldn't ask for a better travel companion. Mary and I have adventured near and far quite happily together—the only caveat being that I drive. Though she is a good driver, Mary has never enjoyed driving and will use any excuse to occupy the passenger seat. Maybe it was my flowery proclamation that I was at her disposal, ready and willing to be her chauffeur and travel companion for as long as we both were able, that solidified our friendship. We still have many more miles to go.

There is one point of contention: Mary accuses me of cheating at Scrabble. Anyone looking through a Scrabble dictionary will find words every bit as creative as mine. That argument stands just about as long as it takes for Mary to whip out her *Webster's*.

For our first birthdays of the new millennium, we decided to have a joint celebration. Our families loved the idea. A few friends focused on the meeting of the "exes" at the party; I hope they weren't disappointed by that nonevent. The party was a smashing success, and I'm holding Mary to the promise of having a joint birthday bash every five years. In retrospect, maybe we should make it every two years, or even every year. After all, we have much to celebrate: great families (including a new great-grandchild for Mary to crow about) and great friends.

In the meantime, we'll talk every day, find things to laugh about, enjoy mutual friends and family, take some trips, and play Scrabble (when I can hide Mary's *Webster's*). Through word and deed, I'll continue to show Mary that I value her presence in my life, and I'll never take our friendship for granted.

—*Beth Lynn Clegg*

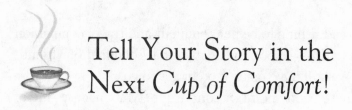

Tell Your Story in the Next *Cup of Comfort*!

We hope you have enjoyed *A Cup of Comfort for Friends* and that you will share it with everyone you know.

You won't want to miss our next heartwarming volumes, *A Cup of Comfort for Inspiration* and *A Cup of Comfort for Christmas*. Look for these new books in your favorite bookstores soon!

We're brewing up lots of other *Cup of Comfort* books and *Cup of Comfort* cookbooks, each filled to the brim with true stories that will touch your heart and soothe your soul. The inspiring tales included in these collections are written by everyday men and women, and we would love to include one of your stories in an upcoming edition of *A Cup of Comfort*.

Do you have a powerful story about an experience that dramatically changed or enhanced your life? A compelling story that can stir our emotions, make us think, and bring us hope? An inspiring story that reveals lessons of humility within a vividly told tale? Tell us your story!

Each *Cup of Comfort* contributor will receive a monetary

fee, author credit, and a complimentary copy of the book. Just e-mail your submission of 1,000 to 2,000 words (one story per e-mail; no attachments, please) to:

cupofcomfort@adamsmedia.com

Or, if e-mail is unavailable to you, send it to:

A Cup of Comfort
Adams Media Corporation
57 Littlefield Street
Avon, Massachusetts 02322

You can submit as many stories as you'd like, for whichever volumes you'd like. Make sure to include your name, address, and other contact information and indicate for which volume you'd like your story to be considered. We also welcome your suggestions or stories for new *Cup of Comfort* themes.

For more information, please visit our Web site: *www.cupofcomfort.com.*

We look forward to sharing many more soothing *Cups of Comfort* with you!

Contributors

Timothy Agnew ("No Uncomfortable Silences") runs a part-time sports medicine practice by day and writes whenever he can. He freelances for several publications and is currently working on a collection of short stories. He lives with his wife, Suzanne, in Sarasota, Florida.

Nancy Baker ("The Tiger and the Butterfly") retired from Texas A&M University in 1999, where she was program coordinator for leadership training. Since retirement, she has pursued her lifelong love of writing and directs the ministry to the sick program at her church. Married for forty-three years, she and her husband have been blessed with three children, eight granddaughters, and three great-grandchildren.

Sarah M. Barnes ("Sitting One Out") writes a monthly column for the *Austin American-Statesman* about the joys and challenges of raising a child with special needs and is writing a book on the same subject. A native Texan, she lives in Austin with her husband, Jim, and daughters Meredith and Caroline.

Joyce Lance Barnett ("Moments in Time") has lived her entire life on the farm where she was born in Mills River, North Carolina. There, she and her husband, Carl, raised their two daughters in a medley of horses, hard work, and mountain grandeur. An artist and writer whose work is inspired by people and landscapes, she is also a caregiver to older and infirm members of her community.

Greg Beatty ("After the Heartache") recently completed a Ph.D. in English at the University of Iowa. He has since moved to the Pacific Northwest, where he writes, teaches for the University of Phoenix Online, and tries to stay out of the rain.

Jason Berzow ("Holy Brothers") is currently pursuing a master's degree in literature at Portland State University. Originally from Plainview, New York, he lives in Portland, Oregon. He has written numerous short stories and poetry, and is currently at work on a novel. This is his first published piece.

Renie Szilak Burghardt ("My Enemy, My Friend") was born in Hungary and immigrated to the United States in 1951. She lives in the country, where she enjoys nature, reading, and family activities. Her writing has been published in numerous magazines and anthologies, including *Whispers from Heaven*, *Listening to the Animals*, and *A Cup of Comfort: Stories That Warm Your Heart, Lift Your Spirit, and Enrich Your Life*.

Christine M. Caldwell ("Summer Solstice") recently completed her first novel, *The Complete Lily Lansing*. A graduate of Rutgers University, Camden, she works as a purchasing agent for an electronics manufacturer. Caldwell lives in New Jersey with her husband, Mark, and her daughters Brooke and Jillian.

Bobbie Christmas ("I'll Give You a Dime") is the founder of Zebra Communications, a publishing consulting firm. She is the compiler of *Purge Your Prose of*

Problems, coauthor of *The Legend of Codfish and Potatoes* with Parliament member Dale Butler, and past president of the Georgia Writers Association. Her writing credits include hundreds of articles and stories in more than forty publications. She resides in Atlanta, Georgia.

Judi Christy ("Tomato Soup on Tuesdays") lives with her husband and their children, Zach and Ericka, in Green, Ohio, where she collects antiques, facilitates a monthly writing workshop, and is a Girl Scout leader. She has worked as a free-lance writer since 1988, writing award-winning fiction as well as numerous videos (including an acclaimed documentary on Goodyear blimps), CD-ROM scripts, speeches, and articles.

Beth Lynn Clegg ("Sacred Vow") is a fourth-generation Texan and retiree with three children, two "in-law" children, three grandchildren, two cats, and many treasured friends. After her retirement, she discovered the joy of writing. She also works part-time for a small software company.

Tisha Coiner ("Thelma Rae") began writing poetry at age twelve and in 1997 received an award from the National Library of Poetry. She now writes articles, short stories, and poetry, primarily for children, and works full-time as a cus-tomer service representative for a medical transportation company. A native Oregonian, this busy single mom of three "fantastic kids" also enjoys camping, flyfishing, and painting.

Marcie Hoye Cumberland ("Drinking Buddies") is a wife, mom, grandma, observer, and writer. She is currently weaving together a mystery saga that entwines the lives of seventeen intriguing, yet familiar, characters. When not writing, she creates Christmas miniatures for dollhouses.

Pat Curtis ("Love Lessons") works part-time in the Christian bookstore, Great Expectations. A mother and grandmother, she lives in Joplin, Missouri, with her husband, Max, and their two Yorkies.

Joie Davidow ("Weezer") founded *L.A. Style*, the award-winning magazine of Los Angeles lifestyle, and cofounded *L.A. Weekly*. In 1995, she launched *Sí* magazine, a national Latino lifestyle publication. She is the author of *Infusions of Healing* and the co-editor, with Esmeralda Santiago, of *Las Christmas* and *Las Mamis: Favorite Latino Authors Remember Their Mothers*.

Kathryn E. Dawson ("A Gift from My Ex") holds a "day job" as a writer/editor for a nonprofit organization in central Ohio. She also loves to write about relationships and other quirky parts of her life. One of her essays appears in *The Walker Within*, an anthology of essays selected from *Walking Magazine*.

Judith E. Dixon ("Love Sees No Color"), a retired nurse and widowed grandmother, is currently indulging a lifelong passion for writing. A long-time resident of Florida, she tutors English, edits a small newspaper, and writes about "anything that needs to be said." She has been published in magazines and online, and has won awards for her fiction, nonfiction, and editorials.

Marcie Eanes ("Side by Side") had a childhood dream: to become a writer. By the age of twenty-three, she'd been published in *Seventeen Magazine*, completed an "outstanding student" internship at *Essence Magazine*, and was working as a newspaper reporter in Michigan. Then a near-fatal car accident sidelined her career for nearly ten years. Today, the Wisconsin-born Eanes lives and works in Los Angeles as a freelance copyeditor, journalist, and poet.

Sharon Elwell ("A Friend in Deed") teaches English as a second language at a community college in Napa, California. She recently developed the curriculum for a three-school grant program for whole-family education. She is the mother of three daughters and the grandmother of six.

Rusty Fischer ("Saint Blanche") is a full-time freelance writer, whose articles, essays, and poems have been published widely in anthologies, national magazines, Internet portals, and online publications. He is the author of several *Buzz On* reference guides as well as *Creative Writing Made Easy*, a bestselling series for writing students and teachers.

Cherri Melton Flinn ("Brian's Gift") was born and raised in rural Indiana. Clinging to her Midwest roots, Flinn resides in southern Illinois with her husband of nineteen years and their three teenage children. She is a freelance writer and the author of *Genealogy Basics Online*.

Lynda Kudelko Foley ("Appearances") is a published writer of folktales, science fiction, and inspirational stories. Her mixed heritage of Polish and Mexican Indian (Zapotec) has inspired her to create modern short stories based on the narratives of her ancestors. She currently lives in Northridge, California, with her husband and two sons.

Pat Friedrich ("One Kid at a Time") lives in Baton Rouge, Louisiana, where she is Dean of Students at Northdale Magnet Academy, a nationally acclaimed alternative high school. Pat has contributed numerous articles to educational magazines, including *School Safety* and *Visions Magazine*. She has just completed her first book, the life story of Leroy Priest Helire.

Corinne Gerson ("My Gardenia Angel") is the author of eleven juvenile novels. This mother of two and "nana" of three lives with her pediatrician husband in Manhattan, where they sorely miss seeing the Twin Towers etch out their part of the sky.

Hanna Bandes Geshelin ("The Old Basque and the Young Jew") is a Westerner who has lived in Massachusetts for more than twenty years. A former librarian of a small college, she now squeezes writing inspirational stories and children's literature in between homemaking, serving as a docent at a local historical museum, and visiting lonely senior citizens.

Arlene M. Gray ("Hiking in a Friend's Footsteps") is a professional quilter, writer, and the proprietor with her husband of a guest farm in Blairsville, Georgia. Her favorite occupation, however, is that of mother and grandmother. She is the author of *An Ordinary Life—Touched by an Extraordinary God*.

Maureen O'Connor Hayden ("A Midwest Miracle") is a reporter at the Evansville (Indiana) *Courier & Press*, where she covers the religion beat. A journalist of twenty years, she's written about an array of issues, from family matters to civic affairs. She lives in Evansville with her husband, Daniel, and their three children, Emily, Elliot, and John Michael.

Theresa Marie Heim ("Angel in Camouflage") is a fiction writer who lives with her husband and new baby in Santa Monica, California. She holds a master's degree in creative writing and has published both fiction and nonfiction pieces in numerous publications.

Suzan L. Jackson ("The Start of a Beautiful Friendship") is a freelance writer specializing in topics related to family, travel, and the outdoors. Her articles have appeared in a variety of magazines, including *Mothering* and *Family Fun*, and she's written a book published by John Wiley & Sons.

Joanne Keaton ("A Degree of Friendship") lives in Indianapolis, Indiana, where she works as an editor and writer. She has a master's degree in English from Butler University. Her passion is vertical racing in skyscrapers, and she has participated in the invitation-only Empire State Building Run-up several times.

Sandy Keefe ("What Dreams Are Made Of") lives in El Dorado Hills, California, with her husband and two daughters, Allie and Shannon. Her older son, Burt, lives in Santa Cruz, California. Sandy is a registered nurse who provides case-management for children with severe disabilities. She enjoys freelance writing for consumer and professional publications.

Rita Marie Keller ("Surprise Party") lives in Carlisle, Pennsylvania, with her husband and three children. A writer "all my life," she founded Cacoethes Scribendi Creative Writing Workshop in 1999, for others with "the writing disease." Her stories have been published in numerous print and electronic publications.

Lauren Kessler ("In Praise of Temporary Friends") directs the graduate program in literary nonfiction at the

University of Oregon. She is the author of nine books, including the *Los Angeles Times* bestseller *The Happy Bottom Club* and *Stubborn Twig*, winner of the Victor Award for best literary nonfiction book of the year.

Donna Marganella ("Friends Are Like Shoes") has published short fiction and nonfiction, and favors humorous essays that reveal truths about contemporary life. By day, Donna is a high-tech marketing manager but fails to see the humor in it. She lives in Carlsbad, California, with her husband, Kevin, who still laughs at her jokes.

Sylvia E. Sheets McDonald ("Breaking the Silence") is a stay-at-home mom to two sons, Evan and Seth, and twin daughters, Sara and Katie. She is a graduate student pursuing a master's degree in counseling and a freelance writer. Her writing, most of which focuses on twin-related research and issues, has been published in various magazines. She lives with her husband and children in south central Ohio.

Kathleen McNamara ("Pass It On") is a fourth-generation Californian who lives in the San Francisco Bay Area. She is a health writer who dabbles in fiber arts and calligraphy. Though no competition for Martha Stewart, she also restores antiques, grows an herb garden, and can't resist hunting for great finds at craft shows, flea markets, and eBay.

Karen McQuestion ("How Jack Got His Groove On") lives in Hartland, Wisconsin, with her husband, Greg, and their three children, Charlie, Maria, and Jack. Her writing has been published in dozens of publications, including *Newsweek*, *Chicago Tribune*, and *Guideposts*.

Lynn Ruth Miller ("The Blarney Stone" and "Providence Provides") teaches adults in San Mateo County, California. She has also worked in public relations and served as the promotions director of the San Francisco International Film Festival. An award-winning fiction writer, journalist, essayist, and columnist, Miller's column, "Thoughts While Walking the Dog," appears regularly in the *Pacifica Tribune*.

Victoria Austen Moon ("My Very Best Friend in the Whole Wide World") is a freelance writer who lives in Louisville, Kentucky, with her architect/musician husband and two cats. She is currently collaborating with her brother on a book about the Christian church and when not writing can be found cooking, daydreaming, or cozying up with a cat, a good book, and a large mug of tea.

Joy Pincus ("Rainy Day Friendship") is a writer and journalist living in central Israel. She works for the Center for Global Research in International Affairs, and is a contributor to *Women's Enews* and the *Jerusalem Post*.

LeAnn R. Ralph ("A Tale of Two Snowflakes") resides in the state of her birth and childhood, Wisconsin. A staff writer for two weekly newspapers, she also writes freelance stories about growing up on a dairy farm that her Norwegian great-grandparents homesteaded in the late 1800s.

Wendy Marvel Redmond ("A Song in My Heart") is a nationally published freelance writer who lives on the Oregon coast. When not writing, Wendy enjoys singing, gardening, and walking on the beach. Her daughters are doing an excellent job of raising Wendy and her husband, Brian.

Billie J. Shelton ("All in the Family") lives with her husband and two children in Iowa, where she writes full-time from her home office. Billie's features, profiles, and photography have appeared in thirty magazines, newspapers, and online publications across the United States. Her most enjoyable "gig" is writing a weekly column, "Serendipity," for a local daily newspaper.

Jen Sotham ("Somebody") spent five years counseling adolescents while developing her writing voice, mostly through song. A full-time writer since October 2000, she works in various media, including film, music, television, and short stories. Jen resides in Astoria, New York.

Sigrid Stark ("My Jar of Self-Esteem") once considered a career as a funeral singer. She now lives in Edmonton, Alberta, Canada, where she juggles being the mother of four teenagers, a pastor's wife, and the manager of marketing and fund development for a local nonprofit. Faith and friendship continue to inspire her writing.

Marcia Tibbo ("True Love in Action") is a native New Zealander who relocated to Australia in 1988, where she continues to live with her young son. A former newspaper reporter, photojournalist, corporate scriptwriter, and desktop publisher, Marcia now works as a freelance writer while she studies creative writing.

John K. Waters ("Bozo") is a Silicon Valley–based freelance journalist and author. His work has appeared in a wide range of publications, including *The San Francisco Examiner* and *Fortune* magazine's *eBusiness* Web site. His books include *The Everything® Computer Book* and *John Chambers and the Cisco Way: The New Laws of Leadership.*

Jae Worth ("Inner Vision") is the pen name for author Janean Nusz, who lives in Kansas with her husband and two children. Her nonfiction articles, on subjects ranging from parenting and budgeting to women's issues, have appeared in a variety of publications. Her published fiction includes *Gryphon's Gold, Moonlight Medallion, Lady Geyr, Lilly Loller's Always Late, Destiny's Promise,* and *Ranger's Way.*

Lou Killian Zywicki ("Dumpster Roses") is a freelance writer and a full-time teacher of writing, literature, and interpersonal communications at the Secondary Technical Center in Duluth, Minnesota. The mother of four children, she lives in a rural nature paradise with her husband, Ernie.

About the Editor

Colleen Sell has long believed in the power of story to connect us with our inner spirits, the Higher Spirit, and one another. Her passion for storytelling was inspired by her mother, who often used stories to guide her young daughter up "fool's hill," that steep climb from adolescence to adulthood. Judging by the stories now being woven by her six-year-old granddaughter, the family legacy of mother-daughter storytelling continues.

The editor of more than fifty published books and the former editor-in-chief of *Biblio: Exploring the World of Books* magazine, Colleen Sell is also an essayist, journalist, screenwriter, and book author. In addition to the books in the *Cup of Comfort* series, her recent credits include *10-Minute Zen* (2002).

She and her husband share a century-old Victorian on forty acres, an original Oregon homestead, which they are renovating and converting to a lavender and Christmas tree farm—an experience that is providing plenty of fodder for many great stories.

Also Available in the . . .

A Cup of Comfort

Stories that warm your
heart, lift your spirit,
and enrich your life

COLLEEN SELL

ISBN: 1-58062-524-X
Trade Paperback, $9.95

The stories in this inspiring collection are pick-me-ups that will soothe and refresh your spirit.

Written by people just like you, these uplifting, true stories take you through some of life's most special moments. You will feel a renewed sense of fulfillment at the joy present in everyday life.

∼ A teacher unknowingly gives two five-year-olds their first birthday party.

∼ A young couple is able to buy their dream house because of the generosity of strangers.

∼ A teenager learns the value of hard work when he spends the summer working for his grandfather.

∼ A despairing single mother rediscovers the blessings in her life because of a special surprise from her six-year-old.

Lie back and relax with a nice, warm
Cup of Comfort!

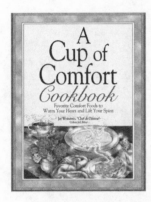